Quinn's Quirks

The rugby wit and wisdom
of Keith Quinn

Quinn's Quirks

The rugby wit and wisdom
of Keith Quinn

TRIO
BOOKS

Front cover illustration: Murray Webb.

National Library of New Zealand Cataloguing-in-Publication Data

Quinn, Keith.
Quinn's Quirks: The rugby wit and wisdom of Keith Quinn / Keith Quinn.
ISBN 978-0-9582839-0-8
1. Quinn, Keith – Anecdotes. 2. Rugby Union football – Anecdotes.
3. Rugby Union football players – Anecdotes. I. Title. 796.333-dc 22

Cover designed by Wakefields Digital for Trio Books Ltd.
Typeset and printed by Astra Print, Wellington.

To the players who play the game of rugby at all levels, and to the referees. They are all the stars of this collection of rugby stories.

Contents

Introduction

In my TV commentary days I had a reputation of sorts for maintaining and using statistics and stories about each player's details and background. Those details were fun to research and use. But commentary styles have changed, even in the past few years. Now, perhaps because of the speed of the modern game, there might be less time to add in the extra information to humanise broadcasts. I have always felt that TV commentary should say something more about a player than just their height, weight and number of tries scored.

Also, in my time as a rugby reporter I always enjoyed listening to players at after-match functions or in conversation, as they recalled incidents from *around* the games they played in. The history of rugby is filled with characters, yarns and memories of hard-case incidents.

This book is the result of the dogged recording of rugby stories in a number of well-thumbed notebooks at my place. Not trusting my memory, after reading or listening to stories I wrote them down for future reference. I have had some of the notebooks for more than 20 years, and many are held together by aging rubber bands. To anyone else my scrawl is indecipherable – sometimes I included only the punch line to an anecdote I had picked up along the way.

This book is an attempt to put the best of those stories together. A number have been published before, and to that end I wish to thank Dave Campbell, editorial director of the excellent New Zealand weekly *Rugby News*. For the past five years he has encouraged me to come up with quirky stories for a column called *Quinntessentials*. I also thank Campbell Burnes, the former Manu Samoa international, who is on the Rugby News editorial staff. Some of the stories have been published elsewhere or talked about on my weekly spot on Radio Sport with my old touring mate, Brendan Telfer. Where needed for the sake of clarity, I have included the year an items was first published.

I would like to thank the following friends and colleagues for their assistance (New Zealanders unless stated otherwise): Clive Akers; H F Boy; Peter Bush; Peter Clark (for his outstanding photos of the "water polo" test at Eden Park in 1975); Frankie Deges, of Argentina; Jeremy Duxbury, of Fiji; Peter FitzSimons, of Australia; Wyn Gruffydd, of Wales;

Peter Kirkwood, of Scotland; Willie Los'e; Peter Marriott; John McBeth; Brian McGuinness; Geoff Miller; Robyn and Avril Murray, of Scotland; Ron Palenski; Peter Sellers; Brian Shennan; Pete Smith; Dick Tayler and Murray Webb, a brilliant caricaturist.

Over the years I have had many excellent published "sources" for stories. In this era where, via the Internet, one can read overseas magazines and newspapers from all over the world every day, I particularly acknowledge the style, substance and humour of *The Sydney Morning Herald*, *The Age of Melbourne*, the Internet sites *Rugby 365* and *Scrum.com*, *The Daily Telegraph* of both Sydney and London, *The Times* of London, *Rugby World* and *NZ Rugby World*. I have read stories in all of those and, where applicable, the punch-line has gone into the scruffy notebooks for future use.

I also have to thank my family for their patience. My wife Anne, and Rowan, Bennett and Claire, and Shelley and Michael. And also our beautiful grandkids, Maggie, aged five (who made it into my notebooks with her descriptive word for a large rugby crowd, "there are a million-pillion people here!"), and four-year-old James, whose first words, I insist, were "crouch, hold, touch... engage!"

From the start the publisher of this work, Trio Books, of Wellington, insisted that there was a book inside the hundreds of notes and scrawl. To that end I thank Phil Murray, Joseph Romanos and Gael Woods for their faith in putting this collection together. It has certainly been fun.

And thanks, too, to the people at Astra Print, especially Christine Borra and Deborah Quin.

Keith Quinn
July, 2007

Colin for comfort

New Zealand-South Africa test matches are no laughing matter. Never have been.

Bruce McLeod, the All Black hooker from 1964-70, told me a story not long before his death in 1996. McLeod — "Angus" to his team-mates — said he always liked to take the field next to Colin Meads. It made him feel more confident to have the indomitable Pinetree nearby.

According to McLeod, the superstition dated back to the fourth test against the Springboks, at Eden Park, in 1965: "There was

Hooker Bruce McLeod (2) liked having Colin Meads around. No wonder — another try for the All Blacks.

a big build-up to the test. They'd won the third test with a big comeback, so the series stood at 2-1 to us before that last match. I was pretty nervous. The players happened to be standing in a line just before running on to Eden Park. I looked across to the Springboks and they looked very big and grim. I whispered to Piney, 'Geez, they look ready'. He never even blinked. He just said, 'I'm f***** ready too'. I felt so good when I heard him say that. I've never forgotten that feeling of comfort."

Joseph Romanos Collection

To Springboks, the feeling going into a test against the All Blacks is equally intense, as is illustrated by this story of Joggie Jansen, the dynamic centre who had such a devastating impact on Brian Lochore's team during the 1970 series in South Africa. Jansen was still on the test scene six years later, when Andy Leslie's All Blacks arrived in South Africa, and was named as a test reserve. During a pre-test photo session, he was asked to smile for the camera. Jansen refused, saying: "You don't smile when you may be playing the All Blacks."

Legal winner

At the 2006 Canterbury Winter Sports Awards dinner, the main award was for the region's Winter Sportsperson of the Year. The winner, quite rightly, went to the one-and-only, the local hero himself: Richie McCaw.

And the prize? Why, $1000 worth of legal fees.

Broadcasting pioneer

In March 2005, Peter Sellers, the distinguished retired radio broadcaster from Dunedin and ever one to set the record straight, sent me the obituary of Alfred Laurie Canter, of Devonport, Auckland. Not only was Mr Canter for 21 years the racing and sports editor of the now-defunct *Weekly News*, he was also the first person to broadcast an All Black test match. Though commentary had been first achieved in Christchurch several years earlier, Mr Canter did "a running commentary" on the All Blacks-Great Britain match in Dunedin in 1930. The first New Zealand telecast of a test was in 1962.

Dark day

The New Zealand-Scotland test at Murrayfield in 1978 has become a classic memory for those of us who were there. We recall the abject gloom in which the all-important game – if the All Blacks won they would complete a historic first Grand Slam of test victories on a tour of Britain – was played. The video footage that remains shows only that it looked extremely dull, but to the 69,000 people at the ground, the rugby was played in near-darkness.

In December in Scotland temperatures can drop very low and are often accompanied by gloomy, foggy weather. December 9, 1978, was just such a day.

On the day before the Saturday fixture the weather was so bleak in Edinburgh there was virtually total darkness by mid-afternoon. As the international the next day was set to kick off at 2.15pm, inquiries were made by television staffers about whether an earlier kick-off time might be contemplated. Murrayfield had no floodlighting then, so this was sound thinking. The no-lights attitude was typical of the conservative nature of Scottish rugby thinking at the time.

There were good reasons for having an earlier kick-off. Back then, television schedules were not jam-packed like they are today. In Britain on the BBC there was a *Grandstand* show that ran all Saturday afternoon, so bringing the game's start time forward would presumably have been a relatively simple matter for the programmers. The BBC could either have shown the game in an earlier time slot or recorded it for replay at its original start time. The other main carrier of the game was Television New Zealand. A 2pm kick-off in Edinburgh was a 2am slot in New Zealand. Therefore shifting the kick-off to midday for BBC (midnight for New Zealand) would have been beneficial.

Even with this sound logic supporting an earlier start, it didn't appear that it was going to happen. So I took it upon myself to phone the Scottish Rugby Union and ask whether they had considered how disastrously gloomy the weather might be by late afternoon. I mentioned that by midday on the Friday it was gloomy enough in Edinburgh for the lights down Princes Street shopping precinct to be switched on fully, and that by 1pm that day the famous Royal Mile could be seen only with the distinctive street lamps showing the way.

The Scottish Rugby Union official who took my call was the secretary, John Law. His tone was short and direct. "Sir," he said frostily, "we are keeping an eye on the weather and if it is dark we will bring the kick-off of the international forward. Don't worry – we are mindful of the situation."

I pressed on and asked: "If you do bring the kick-off forward, by how much will you do it? As a broadcaster for one of the TV stations taking the game I will have to ring my producer in London to alert him to book an earlier satellite time for the transmission." I well remember the curtness of the secretary's reply: "If the weather is exactly like this tomorrow, we will bring the kick-off forward by five minutes."

And, astonishingly, so they did. If anything, the darkness the next day – at not 2.15pm, but 2.10pm! – was worse than it had been the day before.

It got so dark that even the false lightening via the electronic cameras could not disguise the increasing duskiness. The cameras desperately tried to hold on to the last remnants of Edinburgh light that afternoon. A modern comparison of the night-vision of the cameras at Murrayfield would be the images we saw in the gloom of night-time war action in Afghanistan and Iraq, or of the 2007 cricket World Cup final from Barbados.

FOOTNOTE: In 2001, while on holiday in Scotland, I visited some friends I had met on my 1978 visits to Murrayfield. The famous ground was being renovated and the turf replaced. When the Scottish union learned I was coming, several of their staff kindly lifted a slice of the grass and presented it to me in a neat box. It was accompanied by a plaque that read: "On this spot on December 9, 1978, Bruce Robertson scored the winning try for New Zealand in their 18-9 win over Scotland."

It was a humorous and thoughtful gesture and I appreciated it even more when they recruited British Lions player Simon Taylor, who was training there, to present it me. Unfortunately the foot and mouth scare in 2001 prevented me bringing the turf to New Zealand and presenting it to Bruce Robertson.

Because the New Zealand Customs Department would never contemplate allowing the piece of bonny Scotland (being presented, *above*, by Simon Taylor) to be transplanted to New Zealand, it was instead replanted in the front garden at the farm of Avril and Robyn Murray, in Tillicoultry, Clackmannanshire, in central Scotland, near the city Stirling. To this day a small New Zealand flag is planted permanently in the square piece of Murrayfield turf. Mr Murray says: "Any holidaying New Zealanders wishing to see the famous sod are welcome to visit anytime — for a £5 visitor's fee, of course."

Anzac spirit

Thoughts turned to the Anzac spirit in this special week. As recently as 1989 an Anzac rugby team played the British and Irish Lions in Brisbane.

The splendid idea was not entirely embraced by the New Zealand Rugby Union, because only three players were sent to Brisbane to help make up the complement of 22 players to face the Lions. No less than 12 New Zealand players elected not to go, but Kieran Crowley, Frano Botica and Steve McDowell joined such established Wallaby stars as Nick Farr-Jones, David Campese, Michael Lynagh, Simon Poidevin and Steve Cutler.

Before the game three great soldiers, all Victoria Cross winners from Australia and New Zealand, were introduced to the crowd. One was Captain Charles Upham of New Zealand, holder of the VC and Bar. He was followed by that most famous Australian rugby star of the 1930s, Sir Edward ("Weary") Dunlop, also a decorated World War II hero, and the first Victorian player to earn Wallaby honours. The third player was Sir Roden Cutler, a VC winner, former Governor of New South Wales and grandfather of Steve Cutler.

In that 1989 game the Lions beat the Anzacs 19-15.

Many people thought it was the first time an Anzac rugby XV had taken the field. In fact, the acronym was used in a rugby context as far back as 1915, when an "Original" Anzac football team played in Malta. There is neither a written history of the team nor a record of its results. An Anzac team toured Britain at the end of World War I as well, playing many matches in Britain.

1996

Last drag

Is it just me or do the best stories come from tests played in Dublin, Ireland? Former Irish International Willie Duggan used to like the odd drag or two on a cigarette before a test. Once, at Lansdowne Road, as he ran out to play – last in line as usual – he was holding a lit cigarette. As he passed the touchline he said to the referee: "Hey sir, hold this," and pushed the half-finished cigarette into his hand. As BBC television cut to the start of the game the referee could clearly be seen, still holding the glowing cigarette.

And another from the same ground. When the 1997 All Blacks played there, Ireland's hooker and captain was the energetic Keith Wood. The Irish began at a frantic pace and scored a couple of early penalties. The first was after just five minutes and Eric Elwood put his country into the lead. As the teams jogged back to halfway Keith Wood could be seen on television handing an object to referee Tony Spreadbury. It was Wood's wristwatch.

Night-time habits

Can this study possibly be accurate?

It is from a report in London's Daily Telegraph in June 1997. Various women from differing walks of life were asked to sum up the difference between New Zealand and American men. One woman replied: "In America a guy might wake you in the middle of the night to make love. By comparison a Kiwi bloke might wake his woman, but only so that together they could watch the All Blacks play in a live satellite game."

Two tests to be proud of

How about this? There were Quinn and McBeth, after the South Africa-All Black test in Auckland in 2006, two forlorn figures standing in the rain on Sandringham Road, trying to hail a taxi back to town, when a voice boomed out of the darkness: "Want a lift, boys?" It came from a slightly familiar figure walking along the footpath. We gratefully accepted.

The generous Aucklander was none other than the 1977 All Black Colin Farrell, heading home after what he said had been a great weekend. He had been to the All Black dinner on the Friday night, to several other functions as well and was still on a high after the thrill of introducing his 18-year-old son to Colin Meads.

I asked Farrell how he recalled his all-too-brief time as an All Black. He replied: "The two tests I had in 1977 were an experience I'd never want to miss. After that I played in Italy for four years, where Carwyn James' coaching was a big influence. I also had some great years with Auckland in their Ranfurly Shield eras of the 1970s, and played for Auckland against the Springboks in 1981. I remember all my rugby with great satisfaction."

Joseph Romanos Collection

Over the years Colin Farrell has taken some strong criticism from people who forget what a fine fullback he was, deserving of All Black selection. He had only two tests, both against the British Lions, and they were tough games, played in lousy weather. It's great that Colin has such positive memories and has pushed the doubters back to their rightful place.

People sometimes overlook what a fine fullback Colin Farrell was for Auckland.

Pushing the boundaries

Please note that in the evolving English language, as heard on Radio Sport every day, it was New Zealand under-19 coach Aussie McLean who "widened the boundaries". Speaking from France, when being interviewed on the phone by Martin Devlin, McLean was asked how the referees were going about controlling the lineouts at the world under-19 championship. Aussie let rip with a classic bar-room reply: "They're effing crap," he said (with full version of the eff word). He then tried valiantly to correct himself – and Devlin scrambled for the "dump" button – but it was too late. Thus a new era of on-air radio expression was born.

2003

Anonymous All Blacks

Guy Winiata, of Wellington, provided this nice story, which shows that not everyone instantly recognises the world-famous All Blacks. Apparently a Manners Mall hairdresser in Wellington had four men walk in on the Friday before the England-New Zealand game. As she cut each one's hair she offered the usual small talk: Are you from Wellington? Do you like our weather? Are you up for the game? The usual questions.

"Yep," was the answer to each.

"So you play a bit of rugby then?" she asked next. "Yep," was the reply again.

"Who do you play for?" said the hairdresser next. "The All Blacks," came the calm answer.

The hairdresser says she vaguely recognised the four players, but didn't get their names. But she was very nervous with her scissors from then on.

2004

Fleeting fame

Sports fame can be fleeting. Apparently Sir Richard Hadlee was sitting in a café when a wee girl approached and asked if he was famous. "I might be, but don't tell anyone," Sir Richard replied. The excited girl immediately ran back to her parents with the news: "There, I told you it was Andrew Mehrtens!"

Easily mistaken — Richard Hadlee (left) and Andrew Mehrtens.

Fours XV

There's a series of fun trivia quizzes doing the rounds of rugby clubs and sports bars this season. The latest one thrust under my nose is to name an All Black XV chosen from players whose surnames have four letters or less. Here's my best offering: Timu, Lomu, Sims, Rush, Gard, Dunn (either Eddie or Ian), Kirk, Pene, Shaw, Duff, Reid (Tori), Conn, Dowd, Reid (Hika), Bush.

French lessons

C'mon weekend newspaper sub-editors! Surely you can improve on last Sunday's efforts. After the France-New Zealand game the *Sunday News* front-page story ran under a headline of "French Fried", which was apparently to describe a test where the French had a chance of winning right till the end. The *Sunday Star-Times* was slightly closer to the mark with its "…almost French Fried" front-pager. It followed inside with another story headlined "French resistance after Fijian's first half coup". That was okay as a clever play on words to bring in Joe Rokocoko's background.

But the *Sunday News* then took the prize with a "French Dressing" back-page headline on a story by Neil Reid, which included the following sentence: "The All Blacks beat France 31-23 last night – but the win lacked any 'French dressing'."

In view of the change to our prostitution laws last week it's a wonder "French kissing" or "French letters" didn't get a mention.

2003

Towel is back

A note here that the "Crying Towel" is back where it belongs. I'm referring to a famous (or infamous) rugby trophy that is at stake every winter when the Christchurch rugby club plays Linwood.

The "Crying Towel" really is a towel. It was "liberated" by a Christchurch club member in the 1960s. It was actually owned by All Black trialist Brent Elder, who was then about to join the Linwood club. On the towel were the signatures of the 1965 Springbok touring team. When the towel was returned to Elder he noted that the signatures of that year's Christchurch team had been added, and was not impressed.

So the towel was put up as a trophy – to go to the losing team – whenever the clubs' two top teams met. Last weekend, more than 30 years later, Christchurch beat Linwood 19-6 and Roger Mahan, the original liberator, returned from Spain, where he now lives, to present the trophy on behalf of Christchurch. Linwood lost the game, so they are now the holders of a fading but important "crying towel" for another year.

2005

All Black blues

All Black supporters don't take well to their team losing. A loss can swing the mood of the nation. Therefore, the pain must have been deep and soul-searching in 1949, when no fewer than six matches were lost by New Zealand, including two tests on one day.

The All Blacks' top touring party of 30 players went to South Africa that year and, with South African goal-kicking ace Okey Geffin to the fore, were white-washed 4-0 by the Springboks. At the same time a second squad of New Zealand players went down 2-0 to the visiting Wallabies. The six-loss shock was described as the "year of All Black blues". One poet recorded the bleak winter thus:

We'd better face the facts you chaps,
And let the truth be understood,
So let us humbly doff our caps,
For we're no bloomin' good.
Since last July – forget it not –
We've played six tests – and lost the lot.

At New Lands last July, the tale
Was sad when Geffin found his mark;
Last week the final coffin nail
Was sunk on Eden Park.
Forgive if we our teardrops blink –
It's rather tragic – don't you think?

And blame the cooking, blame the chef
The crowds (and don't forget the Press)
The wind, the weather, and the ref,
And biased linesmen – yes.
Such panaceas dim our woe
Just once or twice – but six times? No.

They say confession soothes the soul,
Then banish all the 'buts';
Let's own we lack the right control
And we can't play for nuts.
With all our shortcomings thus confessed
Admit no flowers – by request.

Pass the brick please

The All Black backs passing bricks at a training session in Sydney in 1980 was a diverting sight in the lead-up to the third test. Dave Loveridge's team surely made world history with this approach to the running and passing game.

Ouch – it's the All Bricks

Australian newspapers were fascinated by the All Backs' novel training methods.

It happened after the coach, Eric Watson, and trainer Malcolm Hood decided that the players were not handling the delicate leather rugby ball with enough certainty. The theory of their unusual training was that if the players took care with an object of much greater weight, then passing and catching a rugby ball would be simplicity itself.

What followed was the unusual spectacle of New Zealand footballers, in full training kit, passing bricks from one to another while carefully lapping their practice field.

In Sydney, where the media is so competitive and always on the lookout for some-thing different, the news of the extraordinary training method travelled fast. Soon there were television crews and newspaper photographers in abundance. One newspaper headlined its report: "Look out Australia – here come the All Bricks!"

Did the drastic cure for the fumblers work? That's debatable, because 48 hours later the All Blacks were hammered 26-10 and the test series was lost.

Starting young

Years ago I interviewed Welsh rugby star Cliff Morgan about the game that had taken him away from a potential life of hopelessness working in the coalmines of south Wales to become instead one of the world's finest players and later a leading television commentator.

In his beautiful lilting Welsh accent Cliff said: "I love the sport in my country because of how it grabs us all. In Wales it used to be said that when a baby was born the new parents would lift the swaddling clothes and peer in to see if it was a boy or girl. If it was a boy, it was a tradition for the family to then rush to the kitchen and boil an egg. They would let the egg cool and then put it into the baby boy's hands in the bassinet. That was because it was deemed necessary that from his first hour on God's earth the baby boy could feel the shape of a rugby ball."

1999

The seventh captain

There were five World Cup rugby tournaments from 1987-2003, yet seven captains held up the trophy in triumph. Who were they?

ANSWER: David Kirk and Andy Dalton (New Zealand, 1987), Nick Farr-Jones (Australia, 1991), Francois Pienaar (South Africa, 1995), John Eales (Australia, 1999) and Martin Johnson (England, 2003).

Hold on, you say — that's only six names. The seventh was 1986 All Black captain Jock Hobbs. He was incumbent All Black skipper as the first World Cup approached and was expected to carry on with the job into the new competition. Therefore the New Zealand Rugby Union and its sponsors asked Jock to take part in some pre-tournament photo promotions. One picture taken for Steinlager was of Hobbs holding up the trophy in triumph. The only problem was that only Jock's arms were seen in the shot. He later suffered from concussion and retired before the World Cup. Nevertheless, he qualifies as a skipper who knows the wonderful feeling of holding aloft rugby's greatest prize.

2003

Jock Hobbs lifts the World Cup.

South Australia's rugby connection

When the 1974 All Black team beat South Australia 117-6 in Adelaide, the result was greeted with scorn by the local newspapers in the Australian rules-dominated city. One newspaper captured the feeling well with this heading: "New Zealand All Blacks 117-6. South Australia bats tomorrow".

In fact, among the highest scores New Zealand have registered, four have been against South Australia: 117-6 in 1974, 99-0 in 1984, 77-0 in 1962 and 75-3 in 1980.

Let it not be said that a rugby heart does not beat strongly in South Australia. Balanced against some tough days was a famous 10-7 win by South Australia over Fiji in 1976, their only win over a major rugby country.

Two players from South Australia have represented Australia. The first was Malcolm van Gelder, who rose to prominence while studying at the Royal Military College in Duntroon, near Canberra. Returning to Adelaide, van Gelder, a loose forward, was chosen to tour New Zealand in 1958. He appeared only twice and did not play a test. Then halfback Rod Hauser, a former Queenslander, made the 1973 Australian team for the British tour while studying in the south. After returning to Queensland in 1974 he went on to win 17 caps.

Two other recent promotions showed South Australian rugby in an excellent light. In 2003 the World Cup organisers awarded two games to Adelaide. In the first the Wallabies set a World Cup record for a winning margin when they dispatched Namibia 142-0, and the following day Ireland and Argentina played a thriller, won 16-15 by Ireland. Nearly 60,000 fans watched the two games.

No doubt encouraged by the interest generated by the World Cup games, the South Australian Government and local rugby officials then backed the city to secure a stop on the IRB's world sevens series tour. The first tournament was staged in 2007, when 25,000 fans watched 16 nations play. The Adelaide Oval, long steeped in Australian cricket history, with the Bradman and Chappell grandstands overlooking the action, proved an excellent venue.

South Australian Tourism, perhaps encouraged by the state's New Zealand-born premier, Mike Rann, deemed the occasion such a success it secured the contract to stage the same event till 2011.

Ah, Westport!

I don't generally do jokes – not in everyday life and certainly never a joke of the below-the-belt variety. If there is one thing that an old-time broadcaster can condemn with the advantage of hindsight it is the inclination of today's broadcasters, commentators and talk-show hosts to lower the tone and use inappropriate or tasteless language. As soon as I hear a broadcaster make a sexual innuendo, or an off-colour remark, or a play on words that has a subtle deviance I mentally file that commentator's ability into the bottom drawer.

Having now climbed off my hobby horse, there must be some good jokes around about rugby. Try these…

Did you hear the story of the president of the New Zealand Rugby Union in 1995, Rodney Dawe, of the Buller Rugby Union, when he travelled to South Africa as part of the New Zealand union's social obligations at the World Cup?

As part of his duties Dawe went on to the field at Ellis Park before the final between the All Blacks and the Springboks to assist in introducing the New Zealand team to the South African President, the great Nelson Mandela.

Mandela was the first to speak. He greeted the New Zealander and said: "Hello, I'm Nelson Mandela. I spent 27 years on Robben Island…"

Rodney Dawe looked at Mandela and replied: "That's nothing. I spent all my life in Westport."

Beat this

This joke, for which the name of the rugby team can be changed to suit the story-teller, connects courtroom law with rugby. It's about a small boy who is called to appear in court in front of a judge in a domestic child abuse case.

The judge says to the small boy: "Now you know this is a serious matter. When it's over, which of your parents would you like to live with? Would you like to live with your father?"

"Nooo!" screams the boy. "Not with him. He beats me!"

"Well then," says the judge, "would you like to live with your mother?"

Nooo!" screams the boy again. "Not with her. She beats me!"

"Well," says the judge, "who would you like to live with then?"

"I'd like to live with the Blues rugby team," says the boy, "because they never beat anyone."

Great Gareth

Welsh rugby has its share of stories as well. The great Gareth Edwards was so famous that a bronze statue of him passing the ball was commissioned for the centre-piece of the biggest shopping mall in the centre if Cardiff. It is intriguing that while the Welsh believe Gareth is almost God-like, the great man has always expressed the same opinion about the All Blacks.

Gareth's grandmother lived in a small village in the Swansea Valley and at the height of her grandson's fame she came out of her house and stepped on to an icy footpath. She slipped, hit the ground heavily and was knocked out.

People came running from nearby houses to help and as poor granny was being carried inside, one of the assembled group whispered: "Oh the poor dear, do you think she'll be all right?"

To which a male bystander responded: "Aye, it did look pretty serious, but it could have been worse."

"Worse, how come?"

"Well," said the first man, "it could have been Gareth."

Gareth Edwards, pursued as usual by All Black halfback Sid Going.

Prop's logic

A bright fullback and a prop were having lunch in a smart restaurant. An attractive young waitress approached to take their order. She asked the fullback what he wanted for lunch and he replied: "I'll have the um… healthy salad."

"Very good sir, and what do you want?" she asked the prop.

He looked her in the eye and said: "How 'bout a quickie?"

Taken aback, the waitress slapped his face and said: "I'm shocked and disappointed in you. I thought rugby players these days were high on principles and morality." And with that she departed in a huff.

In the stunned silence that followed, the fullback leaned over and whispered quietly in the prop's ear: "Mate, I think you'll find that is pronounced 'Quiche'."

Stop for red

Another for the Irish jokes column, although British writer Chris Hewitt swears this story is true.

"Before a Six Nations game in Dublin in 2003 the Irish team were based on the outskirts of the city. A police escort involving six high-powered motorbikes was organised to ensure the team had a speedy trip from their hotel to Lansdowne Road. With all the players and officials on board the bus driver moved off. Soon, with police sirens wailing, he was up to full speed.

That is, until the first traffic lights, which turned red as the bus approached. The police bikes went through the red. However, the bus driver slammed on the brakes. The players were catapulted out of their seats and crashed on top of each other.

After the dust had settled, an extremely irate Irish team manager, sprawled in the centre aisle, picked himself up and screamed at the driver: "Why the hell did you stop?" The driver slowly turned and smiled knowingly: "Now listen here, there was no way I was going through a red light with all those police hangin' around."

The fiery Quinn

Let me include at least one personal story in this text. In these days when bosses at radio and television sports stations increasingly turn to former star players to become commentators, the place for the non-star sports broadcaster is disappearing quickly. Career commentators who were not top players are becoming almost a rarity. That is even though in most cases the career commentator might have a far better grasp of what is required at the microphone.

It might be hard to believe but there was a time when I fancied myself as a rugby player who would go on to become a star. I dreamed that it was only a matter of time before my burgeoning talent would explode and I would become an All Black, and a test cricketer too.

I joined the 2ZB radio station sports department in 1967 and bought this grey suit for my first week at work. Forty years later it is true to say the suit would no longer fit.

I can truthfully say I proudly played at lock for Wellington. However, I ought to quickly add that it was for the Wellington Football Club and not for any of our province's teams. I climbed to the giddy heights of the club's senior third team.

After only a few games in that grade it must be said that I started to notice my ambitions and career were starting to level out. I had serious shortcomings as a player. These might have been closely related to poor eyesight and the inability to mix it with any tough-looking opposing players.

However, ego being what it is, I still harboured a need for recognition as a rugby player. For example, I often asked myself why in the reports of our team's games in the weekend newspapers my name was never mentioned. I was playing my heart out in the club's colours but getting no recognition.

Sen Third

Poneke-W'gton

Wellington did not have an easy task running bottom rankers in the competition, Poneke, to a 14-3 win.

Despite a first-minute try by the fiery lock, K Quinn, Wellington had difficulty mastering Poneke in the first half.

Bustling tactics by the Poneke pack, which was playing slightly better than Wellington, paid off when the winger, R Cameron, scored in the corner.

Poneke continued to get its share of possession in the second half, but Wellington, using the advantage of a fairly stiff breeze, badgered them into errors.

So I approached a mate of mine who was a cadet sports writer on the *Sports Post*, the Evening Post's Saturday evening edition, which contained the results of that day's senior games.

One night I asked my reporter mate: "How come when you write up our team's games you never give me a mention? I'm your friend aren't I?" To which my so-called cobber replied: "That's because you're no bloody good."

Not easily discouraged, I shot back: "Listen mate, I know a cub reporter doesn't get paid much. If you give me a decent write-up some time I will pay you with not one, not two, but three jugs of beer." In those days three jugs to us young larrikins was the equivalent of gold nuggets. He gave me an old-fashioned look, which told me he could not be bribed.

Yet the very next Saturday, you guessed it, the *Sports Post* carried a beautiful report on our senior third team's 14-3 win over arch-enemies Poneke. I paid up to my friend and, in fact, gave him a bonus. I had merely hoped for a mention in passing. Never in my wildest dreams could I have hoped to be described as "the fiery K Quinn". Deep down I knew the description was as far from the truth as any words could be. My mate was probably saying through the subtlety of insinuation that I was in fact a pussycat on the field.

Never mind, I have kept the tattered story ever since. It was in my wallet for years. Seeing as the clipping's 40th anni-versary is approaching I re-publish it proudly here. I thank Don Alexander, the writer. I haven't seen Don for years. I hope he enjoyed the beer and has lived life to the fullest.

The game goes on

This is one of my favourite rugby stories. It shows the commitment players of yesteryear had for the game in times when the world around them was crumbling into disarray. War was imminent, but games still had to be played and matches won.

In a mid-week game on the 1914 All Blacks' tour of Australia, New Zealand were playing a Sydney Metropolitan Union XV at the Sydney Sports Ground. During the first half an international telegraph message came into a downtown Sydney Post Office. It was read by the staff and was deemed so important that a small boy was dispatched to cycle with the message to the SCG. The staff knew the message had to be passed on to the biggest crowds of the day.

While the game continued the boy arrived at the ground and passed the message to two other lads who were manning the scoreboard. They in turn climbed the ladder on the front of the scoreboard and alongside the scores of the match in progress they spelt out three words in large letters for all to see. A gasp went up from the crowd of 2000 when the words were noted.

The message on the board simply said: "War is Declared". The players on both teams stopped and read the sobering message. They took in its significance. But in the true spirit of rugby, after a moment's pause, the quiet words of that day's referee jolted the players. The hostilities, which were no doubt to involve both countries, lay in the future. To the task at hand the ref said quietly: "Come on lads, scrum it here… the game goes on."

And it did. New Zealand won 11-6. The record books show that five-eighths Bobby Black and loose forward Jim McNeece were playing in the game and that another forward, Doolan Downing, was in the New Zealand reserves. Within two years all three had lost their lives in Europe, with McNeece dying at Gallipoli only 10 months later. In all, 20 All Blacks died in two world wars.

From the Meads mouth

Legendary All Black lock Colin Meads has always supplied good quotes in his homespun, understated way…

"I can't understand these modern blokes. They don't shave for four days before a test match – and then they go on to the field and try to *look* tough. Instead, why not be like we were in my day as an All Black. Why not have a shave on the day of a test, go on to the field and *be* tough."

―――――――――

"If you're ever going to play good rugby – you'll play it in South Africa."

―――――――――

"I've seen a lot people like him, but they weren't playing on the wing" – in 1995, asked if he'd ever seen a player like Jonah Lomu.

―――――――――

Modern players and coaches are always inventing words when talking about the game. One night Colin Meads was talking to Murray Deaker on Sky TV. Instead of saying "lower socio-economics" it came out as "lower socio-eco systems". That one appealed to me.

Joseph Romanos Collection

The multi-talented and always quotable Colin Meads turns his hand to batting while touring England in 1963. Kel Tremain is wicketkeeper and Mac Herewini is at "suicide corner".

"That was Quinn tonight"

My little personal indulgence to end the year. If you were to ask me for my personal highlight of 2002, would it be seeing New Zealand win the Commonwealth Games sevens gold medal, or watching the same team win the world sevens circuit, or perhaps my own delight in winning a "T P" Lifetime Award for services to journalism in New Zealand? Or what about being the only New Zealand media man to get an eyeball-to-eyeball interview with Vernon Pugh over the NZRFU World Cup cock-ups?

Hell no, none of those things.

Nothing this year compares to the surge of manly pride I felt when a nice lady stumbled over her words while standing at the podium and thanking me in front of 100 women at an education conference in Napier. I had stood in as speaker at the last moment for an unavailable Paul Holmes.

Said the nervous lady to the audience: "... and Keith, you can go back and tell Paul Holmes that here today you comfortably satisfied 100 women in 40 minutes."

2002

Well dackled lads

Broadcaster Willie Los'e was a top rugby player, who played several seasons for Auckland and North Harbour. Willie's biggest moment was when he called on his Tongan family background and made their team for the World Cup in 1995.

With the majority of the squad from "home", Willie struggled to cope when they slipped into their own language. The rest of the team therefore tried to accommodate the non-Tongan speakers. This, says Willie, led to some amusing moments.

"One time we went in to have a pre-game team talk. Our coach, Fakahau Valu, had three 'Ds' written on a large whiteboard. 'These are the key to our game today,' he said. 'The Three Ds. Keep them in mind at all times. They are – defence, distribution and dackle. We must dackle, dackle, dackle anytime anyone in their team has the ball.'"

2003

The inimitable Has Catley.

Counting the cost

Rugby hookers have always been a unique part of the game. But over recent years their role has changed. These days the main role for a hooker is as a foraging loose forward and a lineout thrower. In the old days hookers were dribblers of the ball from around rucks and scrums. They had no role in getting the ball into lineouts. A hooker's absolute priority was to hook the ball in scrums – almost a case for them of "nothing more, nothing less". Not everyone understood the mentality of hookers.

Take the case of Evelyn Haswell Catley, who was a vital part of All Black rugby in the years after World War II. "Has" was always a good, honest hooker. He delighted in keeping a tally of clean hooks and tightheads that he won from his hooking opposite in every game.

Has made his Waikato debut in 1935 and – get this – played first-class rugby over a span of 21 years. His debut for the All Blacks wasn't until after World War II. He was nine days short of his 31st birthday when he made his test debut in 1946, against Australia. His final game was as a 41-year-old in 1956.

Catley loved the battles of being a specialist hooker. He hated yielding any scrum to the opposition. One time in a test the team call was for him *not* to hook in a particular scrum. But he did anyway, and the move took his teammates by surprise. When asked why he had gone against the tactical call not to hook, he reportedly replied: "I had to. My wife was in the grandstand keeping count of the scrums for me." By his wife's count the scrums were won 23-2 and the All Blacks won the game 31-8. But Catley, who had gone against the team plan in just one scrum, was still dropped for the next game.

The shortest reign

How about that 1963 Wellington rugby team? They travelled by train to Auckland for their Ranfurly Shield challenge and had to slosh about Eden Park in the mud for 80 minutes. But the conditions worked in their favour and, captained by Mick Williment, they lifted the shield 8-0. There was quite some party for the winners, and it raged all the way back to Wellington on the overnight train.

No sooner had the triumphant players had their picture taken with the prized trophy on their return than they went a few hundred metres down Lambton Quay to the Midland Hotel. Of course, in those days it was shut on a Sunday. Undeterred, the team banged on the front door of the pub and, upon entering, carried on celebrating for the rest of the day.

On the following day, Monday, there was a civic reception and on Tuesday the full team was hosted splendidly all day at the Wellington Racing Club's midweek winter meeting. Wednesday was recovery day – not from the rugby, but from the excesses of the partying. That meant only Thursday was set aside to prepare for the first shield defence, against Taranaki on the Saturday.

Taranaki, playing to a mean plan of attacking defence, particularly off the back of the lineout, over-ran the sleepy Wellington team. The shield headed to New Plymouth and Wellington's team and fans were left wondering what had happened. The week-long party and lack of practice meant that that tenure was, and remains, the shortest of any Ranfurly Shield era.

Three other Ranfurly Shield curiosities are worth considering.

Which province held the Ranfurly Shield for the longest time? Before you rush to say that Auckland held the famous trophy from September 1985 till September 1993 (eight years, four days), remember this: Southland won the trophy on September 10, 1938, and held it until August 2, 1947, a month short of nine years). Of course, most of the time Southland held the shield play was suspended because of World War II. Instead it sat in the window of H H Geddes Ltd, an Invercargill menswear shop, for nigh on nine years.

Another notable Ranfurly Shield "record" also involved Southland. In 1937 they were shield-holders when they played South Africa. The Springboks won 30-17 and claimed therefore to be mythical holders of New Zealand's beloved Log o' Wood.

Keith Quinn Collection

Short-lived triumph. The Wellington team is proudly welcomed home by Mayor Frank Kitts *(centre, wearing mayoral robes)* and supporters, having lifted the Ranfurly Shield off Auckland. It was gone within a week.

Pacific stalwarts

An honourable mention here of Fijian Waisale Serevi. The great man has played in seven World Cup final events.

Here is Serevi's World Cup record: 1991 (15s, Europe); 1993 (sevens, Edinburgh); 1997 (sevens, Hong Kong); 1999 (15s, Europe); 2001 (sevens, Mar del Plata); 2003 (15s, Australia); 2005 (sevens, Hong Kong).

But by my reckoning one player – also from the Pacific – has bettered even that fantastic record. Brian Lima of Samoa also began in 1991, when he was 18, and hasn't missed a World Cup since. This year's World Cup finals in France will be his fifth in 15s, to go alongside his four sevens tournaments.

31

Public gaffes

The England-France game at the 1995 World Cup was a meaningless third-place clash and both teams looked as if they would rather be elsewhere. At one point the producer of the British ITV coverage was handed a note, which he passed to the commentators to use on air.

The note announced that back in the House of Commons, Prime Minister John Major had announced his resignation. At the rugby in Pretoria, ITV's former England scrumhalf Steve Smith said on air: "Bloody hell, I know this game's boring and England are playing rubbish, but there's no need for the Prime Minister to resign."

A televised game was being played in France on November 11, Armistice Day. The two teams came on to the field in a dignified manner and moved to take up their positions for a minute's silence. The commentator did not exactly cover himself with glory when he said: "Ah, this is a surprise to me. I see they're forming up for a mark of respect for someone. I'm afraid I don't know who has died, but when I find out I'll let you know."

This story is from broadcaster and former Wallaby rugby coach Alan Jones, about former Aussie Prime Minister Malcolm Fraser, for whom Jones once worked.

"One time I went with Fraser to a plush secondary school, one of the best in Sydney for young girls," said Jones. "He was there to present the prizes. The first prize was for English. Up stepped a stunning looking 18-year-old, who approached Mr Fraser and took the prize.

"Then Fraser announced the prize for top in French... and the same stunning looking 18-year-old stepped up and again took the prize. The same thing then happened for top in German, mathematics and history.

"When it came to announcing dux of the school, Prime Minister Fraser announced the winner, and of course it was the same girl. The beautiful lass, in the full bloom of her young loveliness, approached Fraser, who passed over yet another magnificent prize.

"The Prime Minister leaned forward and spoke to the supreme winner. He said to her: 'This is a wonderful thing you've done today. What are you going to do when you leave school?'

"The girl looked at Fraser and fixed her blue eyes on his. "Well," she said sweetly, "I had thought of going straight home..."

Face-to-face

My favourite face-to-face quips from television viewers, and believe me, they all happened…

From an elderly matron: "Hello Mr Quinn, how lovely to meet you. My word, you have improved lately as a commentator. Mind you, you're still bloody awful."

This one from a boy at Rugby Park, Hamilton, one afternoon: "Hi! You're the TV commentator, aren't you?" "Yes," I replied, proudly. To which the boy then said: "My dad thinks you're crap."

And there was the time I was at my beloved Athletic Park in Wellington, waiting by the cameras to do a live report, when I noticed a man of senior years standing nearby and appearing to be watching closely. Eventually I nodded and said a polite "hello" to him. His reply was slightly off-putting. He said: "My God – fancy seeing you. I haven't seen you in the flesh before. You know what I'd do if I was home now? I'd turn you off."

Where's a gun?

Another excellent, if somewhat outrageous, rugby quote from Britain. Leo Cullen, the big Dubliner from Blackrock College, made his test debut in New Zealand last year and has been in the Irish squad ever since. He has steadily built his tally of test caps, though mainly as a substitute player. Then, out of the blue, he was dropped from the squad of 22 to play England in the grand finale of the Six Nations championship in Dublin.

A disappointed Cullen said to the media: "As much as I would have liked to hire a sniper to take out somebody in the chosen squad before the England game, I sensed it probably wasn't the best course of action to take!"

2003

Get me a pie, boy

This great yarn was told by Gary Whetton at a Pakels New Zealand Pie awards dinner in Auckland. Gary told the black-tie dinner: "I was just a kid on tour in Australia. I was in the New Zealand Colts team and we played the curtain-raiser to the All Black game in Canberra." When the Colts game ended Gary sat with the All Black reserves, alongside Andy Haden, his mentor from the Auckland rugby scene, who was in the reserves that day.

After the game had been going for some time Haden whispered to Whetton: "I hate being a reserve. I'm cold, bored and hungry. Let's go back into the warm dressing room and sit there. Maybe you could go and get me a cup of tea. I'm not likely to be needed here. And can you get me a pie as well? In fact, I'm bloody hungry – can you get me two pies please?"

Murray Webb

The young and keen Whetton, not yet an All Black, was only too pleased to oblige and soon Haden had a piping hot cup of tea and two meat pies thrust into his hands. Outside, the game raged. Haden sat in the dressing room, sipping his team and wolfing down the two pies. Whetton kept watch on the door.

But – you guessed it. One of the All Blacks forwards went down with an injury. All Black coach Eric Watson stood up and looked along the line of reserves. "Where's Andy? Find Andy and tell him to warm up – he's on *now!*"

Gary Whetton.

At that point Haden was just completing his second pie and was washing it down with the tea. Watson approached the dressing room. Whetton signalled urgently to Haden what had happened. The great All Black backed into a toilet stall as Watson burst in. He thundered: "Where's Andy?" Then, seeing Whetton, he fixed his eye on him and said: "And what are you doing in the All Black dressing room?"

For a moment things looked bad for Whetton. His chances of becoming an All Black were sinking by the second. Being caught rifling through the All Blacks' private things wouldn't look good for the lad. However, this Keystone Cops situation was saved by Honest Andy. He emerged from the toilet cubicle and, although he initially feigned illness, he did take the field and play the rest of the game. Whetton concluded his tale to the dinner crowd by saying: "Um, I had seen Andy play better than he did that day…!"

2001

Andy Haden. A matter of All Black pecking order.

Mossie mayhem

The Irish and British Lions lock Moss Keane remains one of those hard-case classic men who adorn rugby history. Stories abound about "Mossie".

One time he confessed to being extremely naïve and raw in his younger years. He believed it was because he came from a small country town. "When I went to New Zealand in 1977 I had no idea about rugby," he said. "Out there with the Lions I used to jump in the scrums and push in the lineouts!"

Keane was part of the famous Munster team that beat the 1978 All Blacks. Moss once told me: "That was feckin' amazin'. The final score was 12-0 to us, but 31-6 to them in the lineouts! At the end of the game I went up to Andy Haden to shake his hand. I said to him, 'Hey Andy, we're not used to this winnin'. We're used to losing to you guys. We could write a feckin' thesis about this today.'"

In my time I saw Moss in many different situations. Many of those involved the consumption of the sponsor's products. It was rumoured he downed 30 pints in Auckland the night before the 1987 World Cup final. After one raucous night in Suva his team-mates threw him into the hotel swimming pool. Everyone stood on the side of the pool and roared with laughter at poor Mossie's plight. It was only when it was pointed out that he wasn't coming up from his unsightly plunge that his mates went to his rescue. Moss had never been near water in his life.

And here is former All Black Frank Oliver's story about marking Keane in a test against Ireland in the 1970s. "We were trying to work out the Irish lineout calls, but we weren't doing very well. However, we were helped when we got to one lineout and heard the Irish halfback, as usual, call out a sequence of secret numbers. I was marking Moss and heard him say, 'Oh Jaysus, not to me again!'"

Mossie's parents bought their first television set in 1974, to watch their son make his Irish test debut in Dublin. They were from Kerry, where Gaelic Football is the top game, and had never seen their son play rugby. Moss recalled their reaction to at last seeing their son play the game that had made him famous: "Geez, mum and dad were different. They watched together but took completely different viewpoints. Mother said, 'I'm terrified he'll break a leg'. Dad said, 'He might, but it won't be his own!'"

A rugby toast

Here's to the men with cauliflower ears,
And the great games played in all of their years.

Here's to the oval ball and its beautiful bounce,
To wingers who run and tacklers who pounce.

Here's to mud in your eye,
The wind and the rain, and the sun in the sky.

Here's to referees and the whistles they blow,
And the calls they hear, to "let the game flow".

Here's to a hearty three cheers, after blood sweat and tears…
Here's to swapping shirts – and a shower that works!

Anonymous

2000

No prayers for Peace

Since 1922 the Auckland club final has been played for the Gallaher Shield. The competition continued during World War II and in 1940 the final, between Takapuna and Marist, was refereed by a man named George Peace. When Takapuna won the game the Marist players and supporters were very bitter about Mr Peace's performance. They thought he had whistled their team out of the game. There was an indication of how strong Marist feelings were at Mass the next morning.

Every week in those difficult years prayers were offered from the pulpit for the brave servicemen overseas and for a quick end to the hostilities. But the morning after the Gallaher Shield final the priest at one Auckland Catholic church made a popular decision – he announced that "because of happenings at Eden Park yesterday there will be no prayers for Peace today!"

Hard man Frank

And while mentioning Frank Oliver, the father of Anton, let's not forget he was also an All Black test captain. Frank was a hard man and he had a tussle or two on the field in his time. At one point in an Otago-Wellington clash at Athletic Park a fight broke out between Oliver and Wellington's Brendan Gard'ner. Huge punches were traded. In the end Gard'ner had to leave the field groggy. Two minutes later Oliver also left the field – his injury was a broken hand.

Underneath the grandstand officials decided to send the two players to Wellington Hospital and, ever frugal, bundled the two men off in the same taxi.

Selector McBeth

My television colleague John McBeth insists that he once had a hand in choosing an All Black test team. It was on the tour of Argentina in 1991. The All Black props, Steve McDowell and Richard Loe, had performed disappointingly in the first test and coach Alex Wyllie decided to give them a rocket before the second test. Wyllie mulled over how to do this effectively with several of the touring news media. McBeth says it was he who suggested to Wyllie that McDowell and Loe should be bracketed with their understudies, Graham Purvis and Laurence Hullena, at the announcement of the team for the second test.

It worked. Apparently the two test regulars blinked and swallowed hard when the team for the second test was announced. They saw that their coach was seriously considering making changes in the front row. McBeth says jubilantly that the two veterans trained furiously all week, then played like maniacs in the test, where the All Blacks ran out comfortable winners.

All Black coach Alex Wyllie. Was it true that John McBeth helped him to select one All Black team?

North goes South

Another delightful little refereeing tale. In 1947 Otago held the Ranfurly Shield and Auckland travelled south to Carisbrook to challenge. In those days a referee from a neighbouring region was used to control shield matches. As the most prominent nearby ref at the time was Invercargill's Jack North, he was given control of the big match.

The final score was 31-12 to Otago. The Aucklanders were naturally disappointed and, worse, they felt the refereeing was very "localised". Their hurt feelings were summed up perfectly by an Auckland newspaper report, which suggested in a summary of the game that as a result of his performance with the whistle Mr North's name should be changed – to Mr South.

First telecast

I'm often asked about the first telecast of rugby in New Zealand. It was of a match between the Barbarians club of New Zealand and Waihi Sub-Union on July 25, 1954. This was about six years before home television arrived in this country.

The telecast was put on by Pye (New Zealand) Ltd as an "open-circuit telecast" experiment. There was only one camera and it operated from one side of the field and relayed pictures to a number of 17-inch receivers situated on the backs of trucks that could be seen from the grandstand.

In addition, 14 homes in Waihi were loaned television sets to allow them to follow the telecast. It is not known whether there was a commentator.

Knight-knight

Rugby statistician Geoff Miller, ever a man with an eye for the unusual, points out that there was a very significant front-row in action during a Ranfurly Shield match in 1954. Waikato challenged Canterbury and the result was a 6-6 draw. Opposing each other that day were Jim Stewart, of Canterbury, and Jim Graham, of Waikato. Both were later knighted, Stewart for services to education and Graham for services to agriculture.

Tries not enough

In the 1990s Auckland lost the Ranfurly Shield twice to Waikato on Eden Park. In the first loss, in 1993, Auckland could not score a try and Waikato won 17-6. But how many tries did Auckland score when they lost the shield to Waikato in 1997?

ANSWER: Auckland scored five tries in losing the 1997 game 29-31. Waikato scored only three tries but kicked more goals.

1997

First night game

With all the talk these days about night rugby in Super 12 and test matches, it's worth harking back to the first floodlit rep rugby game played in this country. It was played by North Auckland and an Auckland XV at Rugby Park in Whangarei on May 7, 1955.

Kick-off was at 9.15pm, much later than night matches these days, and the result favoured North Auckland 19-3.

The first night rugby game was played in England, when Broughton met Swinton at Broughton in 1878. The lighting used was from two "Gramme's Lights" mounted atop 30-foot poles. Progress was swift in improving lighting – later that season a game was played under the illumination of two Siemens "electro-dynamo" machines, each with four lamps.

The best story about the early days of floodlit rugby comes from Hawick, in Scotland, where 5000 fans were present in 1879 for a local derby against neighbours Melrose.

Apparently many of the locals regarded the semi-darkness of the outer edges of Buccleuch Park as an opportunity to see the game for free. The club officials were not impressed, but were reluctant to stop the game, especially because the players were doing their best and snow was falling. And Hawick were winning!

As soon as the game ended the officials had their revenge. They immediately switched off the floodlights, plunging the ground into Scottish mid-winter darkness. The crowd screamed and yelled as they slithered and slid all over each other in the slush underfoot.

Victorious pair

Name the two players who captained the All Blacks to test victories and also captained teams that beat the All Blacks.

ANSWER: Bob Duff and Colin Meads.

Duff captained New Zealand in the third and fourth tests against South Africa in 1956, but did not tour with the All Blacks to Australia in 1957. Instead, when the team returned unbeat-en, a welcome-home game was arranged against Canterbury at Lancaster Park. Duff led the Red and Blacks to an 11-9 victory.

Meads captained the President's XV to a win over the All Blacks in a special internal tour game at Wellington in 1973, two years after he had retired from test rugby.

Canterbury's Bob Duff *(left)* and the All Blacks' Ponty Reid lead their teams on to the field at Lancaster Park in 1957.

Colin Meads is "chaired" from the field after leading the President's XV to victory over the All Blacks at Athletic Park in 1973. The players carrying Meads are *(from left)* Grahame Thorne, South African Albie Bates, Fiji's Vuniara Varo and Brian Lochore.

The great Sean F...

Now that the great man has retired, let me repeat my favourite Sean Fitzpatrick story.

It happened during the World Cup in South Africa in 1995, when Jonah Lomu became a sensation with the fans. The All Blacks were making a promotional visit to a local shop and Fitzpatrick was among the first to arrive. He and the others who followed were mobbed by people asking that all manner of items be autographed.

An elderly lady approached Fitzy and offered a new ball and a pen, saying: "I only want two players' autographs on this ball today." Sean started to oblige cheerfully, but as he began writing his name the massive figure of Jonah appeared behind him.

At that, the woman screamed, grabbed pen and ball and pushed past for her second signature. Fitzy recalls: "If she only wanted two signatures, then somewhere in South Africa there is a ball with two names on it. They are 'Jonah Lomu' and 'Sean F'."

Rugby, league

The Marist club in Auckland has a fine clubhouse and has kept meticulous records from its illustrious past. It is recorded that one of the club's members, the late Dick Ross, can claim a unique place in New Zealand rugby.

Regardless of whether he was permitted to, in a season soon after World War II Ross was still playing rugby union and rugby league in Marist colours. It is even recorded that once he marked two current New Zealand captains on the same day.

In the morning he played rugby union against Grammar and marked All Black captain Fred Allen. That afternoon he turned out for the Marist rugby league team and came up against Kiwis captain Robbie Robertson, who played for Richmond.

Perks of the job

This pre-historic scaffolding at Buckhurst Park, Suva, in 1977 tested the courage of petrified commentators. The wind blew off the sea and the scaffolding shook wildly for the Keith Quinn descent. But it was okay — the structure was held up by string and camera cables!

Did you know?

Brothers Stephen and Graeme Bachop achieved a world first by playing against each other for two separate countries – Samoa and Japan. That was years after they had played together for New Zealand.

John Schuster returned to the Samoan team to play his second test for them, 13 years after his first appearance.

Ili Tabua, of Fiji, played for his country at the 1999 World Cup after appearing for them in 1989-90 under another version of his family name, Ilivasi Tamanivula. He also played 10 tests for Australia from 1993-95.

Two players who had the same Christian and surname opposed each other in a test match – Greg Smith for Japan met Greg Smith for Fiji.

The record for most players of the same Christian and surname appearing in the same test match is three – John Williams, in three British Isles v South Africa tests in 1974. The commentators' nightmares were eased by calling the players "JPR" and "JJ" for the British Isles, and "John" Williams for South Africa.

Three New Zealand-born brothers played for different countries: Steve Gordon played for New Zealand; Rob Gordon played for New Zealand and Japan; and John Gordon played for Canada and Hong Kong.

Young Ted

Several people have asked why Graham Henry's lifelong nickname of "Ted" was never explained before he left for Wales.

He recently related how he had been called Ted since his childhood days. Apparently as a lad Graham helped run the cricket scoreboard at Lancaster Park in Christchurch. The scorer, who had been there for decades, was known as "Old Ted" to all and sundry. So the lad helping him so keenly was soon dubbed "Young Ted". The name stuck.

A supporters' group of two

No doubt there are at present hundreds of rugby-mad New Zealanders in tour groups following the All Blacks around Britain and Ireland. The number of these supporters has always been guessed at – in 1996 it was estimated there were 5000 Kiwis following the All Blacks in South Africa, and one year recently about 20,000 went to Melbourne to watch the Bledisloe Cup game.

Travel being more difficult and money being tight back in the good old days, the support group following the 1935-36 All Black tour of Britain numbered – wait for it – just two.

They were Mr Pat Barry and Mr Donald Small. Everywhere they went local fans and officials fêted them. In the end the All Black team accorded the pair a kind of official status. They were each given a team blazer, were invited to every after-match dinner and listed in local guides as either "All Blacks" or "Members of the New Zealand Party".

Tight-lipped

The quote of the last week goes to All Black coach John Mitchell, speaking about the announcement of his two assistant selectors, Mark Shaw and Kieran Crowley. Asked whether the two would be talkative types like some selectors we've had in the past, Mitchell remarked: "I don't think they'll be too expansive with their words."

What an understatement sir! Crowley has long been considered a strong, silent farming type and in his playing days was far from loquacious in the company of the news media. And as for Mark "Cowboy" Shaw, he quickly gained a reputation during his All Black days for often not going beyond one syllable words in a full conversation, especially on test days. He was always the epitome of the strong, silent type of All Black.

On one of his All Black tours, I well recall Shaw's paucity of vocabulary, or at least his unwillingness to dip into it. I was

Joseph Romanos Collection

positioned at a nearby breakfast table and over-heard a conversation from Shaw that went something like this:

WAITRESS: "Are you having breakfast, sir?"

SHAW: "Yep, ta."

WAITRESS: "And will you be having tea or coffee, sir?"

SHAW: "Yep, tea, ta."

WAITRESS: "And what will you be having with that, sir?"

SHAW: "Toast, please, ta."

WAITRESS: "Will that be all, sir?"

SHAW: "Yep, ta."

2002

Mark Shaw — tight-lipped.

Lip service

Here's another colourful story from *Rugby Almanack* editor Clive Akers' stash of rugby memories. It concerns 1904 All Black halfback Patrick ("Peter") Harvey. He played one test, against the touring British team, and had high hopes of making the New Zealand team for the massive world tour that was to follow in 1905-06 – the team that was later to become known as "The Originals" and was the first to be known as "the All Blacks".

Harvey's strong play as a halfback duly earned him selection for that trip. But he never made it. His employment was as a lip-reading teacher at the School for the Deaf in Sumner, Christchurch. His application for leave to enable him to tour became a hot issue and went to Parliament for a final ruling. The Prime Minister, Richard John Seddon, became involved and he ruled that because Harvey was the only teacher of his type in the country he could not be spared for the rugby.

So Harvey's All Black career ended. As one report put it: "He was never heard of again."

Doctor sees yellow

Another famous first for rugby occurred last week. During an international game a team doctor was shown a yellow card and dismissed from the field. It came at Witbank, in the midweek game of Argentina's South Africa tour. The doctor was Argentina's Mario Larrain and the referee was Jamiel Panday, of South Africa. Apparently the referee judged that the doctor was on the field at an inopportune time – while a goal kick was being taken – and so the yellow card was shown.

When asked about the incident afterwards the Argentinian doctor raised a good point. "Yes," he said, "this is a very interesting case. But are they now going to allow replacement doctors when one gets yellow-carded? After all, we have a specialist position in a game, like a prop does."

2002

They said it

"I'm gutted, absolutely devastated. But I'm not down." – *All Black winger John Kirwan, after his sensational dumping from the All Blacks in 1993.*

"We've never been in the record books, so this was our chance." – *Marlborough rugby captain Frank Marfell, whose team lost 128-0 to Western Samoa in 1993.*

"The French are predictably unpredictable." – *Andrew Mehrtens, after the All Blacks' surprise loss to France in the 1999 World Cup.*

"For an 18-month suspension, I feel I probably should have torn it off. Then at least I could say, 'Look, I've returned to South Africa with the guy's ear'." – *Johan le Roux, after biting Sean Fitzpatrick's ear in 1994.*

"I prefer rugby to soccer. I enjoy the violence in rugby, except when they start biting each other's ears off." – *Actress Elizabeth Taylor in 1972.*

"I asked them to make me an offer I couldn't refuse, and they did." – *All Black fullback John Gallagher explains why he signed to play league for Leeds in 1990.*

"You don't look big enough to be a rugby player." – *The Queen, when presenting former All Black captain David Kirk with his MBE.*

"The weakest team New Zealand has ever had... weak in the scrums, weak on defence and lacking in pace sums up the team." – *Former All Black hooker George Tyler, writing in the New Zealand Herald about the 1924-25 New Zealand side about to leave for Britain. They returned unbeaten and have become known as "The Invincibles".*

Murky depths

Each year there is a Front-Rowers lunch in Sydney and last week one of the star turns was the crafty old campaigner of the 1970s, Stan Pilecki. Big Stan spoke mostly about life in the murky world of scrummaging. He also spoke about smoking and how it related to props. Stan used to enjoy a last fag minutes

Two tough old Wallaby forwards, Tony Shaw (left) and Stan Pilecki.

before running on to the field. "In fact," Pilecki told the Sydney crowd, "one of the most difficult things I found in rugby was learning how to stamp out a cigarette with your boots on!"

Also from Australia, John Eales has a good front row story about composure on the field. Eales reckons that one time in Ireland a rugged prop had listened before a game to his coach, who was emphasising how important composure would be in the upcoming game.

But soon after kick-off the prop punched an opponent and was sent off.

His coach was furious. He said: "I told you not to fight today. I asked you to keep your composure. What happened?"

The prop replied: "Well, in the first scrum my opposite told me he was going to hump my sister tonight, so I clunked him."

"But," said the coach, "you haven't got a sister."

"I know," said the big Irishman. "I was thinkin' that as I walked off!"

2003

Clubhouse classics

Now that club rugby has started all over the country it is time to remember all the selfless people who offer so much support to the club teams and the schoolkids who battle it out week after week, rain, hail or snow. All power to them!

In tribute to lower-grade rugby players I offer my 10 Most Over-used Statements heard in rugby clubhouses each winter:
1. I thought you said we'd have no trouble finding the ground.
2. I've always said your son is going to be a great player.
3. No, I reckon you're playing as well as ever.
4. You're one of the best I've ever seen under the high ball.
5. Thanks ref. You controlled the game to the best of your ability.
6. Didn't you hear me say "yours"?
7. The coach just said you'll definitely get a game next week.
8. That bloke I marked today was scared stiff of me all game.
9. Honest, the sun was in my eyes.
10. You played really well today, er, can I have a ride home please?

2003

Keeping it Kiwi

Word of the year on television? It has to be "hoiking", as used by referee Steve Walsh when we eavesdropped on his microphone during the televised Northland-Southland game in Invercargill. Mr Walsh used the word when he called the captains together and told them he objected to bits of flying spittle landing on him after a Southland player spat at one of the Northland boys.

In my dictionary "hoiking" is described as "the clearing of one's throat" or, when used as a noun, a "hoick" is a "gob of phlegm". The word in association with spitting is not found in my English dictionaries.

So well done Steve Walsh for keeping it Kiwi!

2002

Rugby Spike

Joseph Romanos Collection

Spike Milligan – rugby fan.

Rugby fans all over the world will be saddened to learn this week of the death of great comedian Spike Milligan. Not everyone knows that Spike was a rugby man. He loved Ireland, of course, but he also had a great fondness for the All Blacks. He befriended several members of the 1972-73 team – in particular Grant Batty and Joe Karam – on their tour of Britain.

This week Earle Kirton recalled the time he was working for the BBC and watched New Zealand play England. Afterwards, in a Dublin Hotel bar, Spike decided that seeing he hadn't ever had the satisfaction of tackling an All Black on the field, he would try it in the bar. He chose Ian Kirkpatrick, the New Zealand captain.

From behind, Spike launched his light frame at the massive Kirkpatrick. Kirton said that it was a genuine attempt at a tackle by Spike, but that Kirky was not jolted enough to spill a single drop of the drink he was holding.

And then there was the time Spike was ushered into the headquarters of the New Zealand Rugby Union, in Wellington. Standing in a smart safari suit and hat, Spike was presented by the secretary of the union at that time, Barry Usmar, with an All Black tie. Spike accepted the gift with great solemnity, but, having no other place to wear it, he then grandly tied it around his hat!

2002

Big blue bull

The Nickname of the Week award goes to Fox TV's commentators, Greg Clark, Phil Kearns and Greg Martin, for naming the Waratahs' red-headed replacement forward Steve Talbot as "the one they call the Blue Ribbon Blue Bull! They only bring him out for the big shows."

2002

All Black memories

I love the way every All Black, no matter how major or minor his career, always gets an obituary published. It is one of our best and most enduring rugby traditions. And usually within each obit, no matter how small, there is a story or two that goes beyond the mere statistics of the man's career.

The recent deaths of 1947-51 All Black forward Lachie Grant, of South Canterbury, and 1953-54 All Black Jack Kelly, of Auckland, reminded me of couple of good stories.

Lachie Grant was a tall, upright man who lived his life with the nickname "Goldie", so Jeff Wilson wasn't the first All Black to have such a moniker. How Grant obtained his nickname was always confusing, given that in his prime his hair was jet black. At his funeral in 2002 it was revealed that as an infant his hair grew in fair and golden, hence the name Goldie. It was only in adulthood that his hair colour changed. But the nickname didn't.

Sir Terry McLean told me that Goldie Grant was an excellent, athletic, lineout man. "That was when lineouts were lineouts," Terry added with a sigh.

I didn't know Jack Kelly well, but he told me one story that is worth recording. Once, back in the 1950s, he was in an Auckland rep team flying home after playing an away match. At the airport there was one too few seats on the plane to accommodate all the players and officials. So the innovative Aucklanders chose the smallest player to hide under one of the seats. Jack felt that from memory it might have been little Grafton halfback Garth Kearney.

Apparently in the Dakota planes there was room for a small person to be concealed. All that was needed was a blanket and the ability to distract the travelling cabin staff.

Chewing it over

Wasn't that a great television shot of the Hurricanes manager Tony Bedford during last Friday night's game in Dunedin. Taken in close-up from side-on, the grinding speed with which the ever-efficient, ever-friendly Bedford's jaw was working was amazing to see. He was anxiously chewing the hell out of a stick of gum as the Hurricanes-Highlanders battle headed towards its most exciting point.

I mention it only because you don't see gum-chewing like that in rugby any more. And quite right too. For safety reasons and all that.

But it was different in the old days. We are told most members of the 1905 All Blacks chewed gum on the field in every match, while "Bull" Irvine, of the 1924-25 team, used to intimidate his opponent by cleverly making use of chewing gum. The crafty All Black front-rower would enter the field chewing a softened, healthy wad of the sticky stuff, and then, at an early scrum, he would jam it in the hair growing in his opponent's arm-pit.

2002

Lights out

This story from the 1935-36 All Black fullback Mike Gilbert. In his later years, when he was confined to a wheelchair, Mike became something of a phone freak, calling all and sundry for a wee chat. And very pleasant chats they were.

Apparently, on the 1935 tour to Britain and France, the manager was the autocratic Vincent (later Sir Vincent) Meredith. He insisted that the night before a game team members had to be in bed by 10.30pm.

Mike used to say: "… and Mr Meredith policed the rule vigorously. He often would do room checks to see if the occupants were tucked up tight by the allowed time. We'd be lying there and suddenly the room door would be flung open and there would be our manager looking in."

Mike claimed that one All Black was dropped from a test for breaking curfew.

He also said that Meredith banned the team from doing the haka on the field. "We don't want to look like a bunch of whirling dervishes," Meredith would say.

The water polo test

A significant anniversary passed virtually unnoticed recently. I thought about it when I saw the weather bomb hit Auckland last Thursday. It crossed my mind that possibly there hadn't been rain in the city that heavy for exactly 27 years. On June 14, 1975, the heavens opened for 48 hours and such was the deluge that the All Blacks-Scotland test was in danger of being cancelled. The game did go ahead, and the images of the flooded field are a reminder of the wettest conditions in which a test has been played in this country. The game is now often referred to as the "water polo test". All Black prop Billy Bush told me once he feared players might drown in collapsed scrums or rucks.

2002

You can see why New Zealand-Scotland, 1975, was dubbed the "water polo" match. This photo was taken hours before the tide was at its highest.

The TV crews almost had to claim off-shore travel for working in these conditions.

Office burgled, tickets safe

Here's a crime story with a *really* happy ending. It happened last week when a prominent Wellington businessman had his sleep disturbed by his security company phoning to say his city office had been broken into. "What's been taken?" asked the sleepy businessman. "Well, I can see a laptop has gone off a desk, but you'd better come in," said the security man. "Your office here is a bit of a mess."

So the sleepy boss headed towards the city. Halfway through his journey he was suddenly gripped with a much deeper concern, a real panic attack, in fact. He put his foot down.

But arriving at his office, his worries lifted. Sure, his laptop was gone, plus a few other odds and ends, but on his desk, lying untouched, were the 25 test tickets for the Springbok-All Blacks test that he had bought the previous afternoon.

2002

Don't leave a message

Big Colin "Pinetree" Meads appeared on TV1 the other afternoon and faced the usual questions about his career from yours truly and John McBeth. Nothing wrong with going over old ground I suppose, but I wanted to test the big man with a few new questions. In case you missed the sequence, here's how it went:

KQ: Colin, give me some very short answers to the following questions. Do you have a cellphone?

MEADS: Yes, but don't leave me a message, because I don't know how to retrieve them.

KQ: Can you pre-set your video to record a programme?

MEADS: No.

KQ: Do you use an ATM money machine?

MEADS: No.

KQ: Do you ever go to the races?

MEADS: Yes.

KQ: When you come home from an overseas trip, what's your favourite home dinner?

MEADS: Mutton and vegetables.

KQ: Would you ever wear gloves on a rugby field?

Colin Meads — mutton and vegetables, thanks.

MEADS: If it made me a better player, yes.

KQ: How happy are you that we've just heard King Country beat Wanganui today?

MEADS: Bloody delighted!

2001

A pair of dismissals

The phone rang at my place the other night and on the line was that good and loyal rugby man Bill Freeman, asking: "Who was the Wellington player sent off in two Ranfurly Shield challenges?" The question stumped me.

Bill rang back a couple of days later to inform me that he had found out that the player was Huia Gordon, who was dismissed during the Wellington challenge at Eden Park in 1989 and then in the 1993 challenge at the same ground.

Over the next few days several other people asked me the same question, so it's obviously doing the rounds on some sort of sports trivia circuit.

The two instances of Huia Gordon being sent off are intriguing. In 1989 he was sent off by Keith Lawrence in the last minute of the game, Mr Lawrence apparently having had enough of front row wrangling between the teams. And in the second challenge, it was reported in *Rugby News* that Gordon was red-carded by Canterbury's Mike Fitzgibbon for "chipping at a touch judge" while sitting in the sin bin!

2000

Short fall

A good quote this, from *The Times* of London the other day. Columnist Nigel Botherway reported on a session of team bonding exercises called for by Dean Richards, the Leicester Tigers coach.

Things went downhill for the "Leicester Lip", England and British Lions utility back Austin Healey. He fell off a ladder and injured his ankle while learning how to rescue a cat from a roof. Asked by a journalist how far the controversial Healey had fallen, a team-mate replied: "Obviously not far enough."

2000

A trial for the trialists

Any leading New Zealand players who complain about their lot might like to read about the arrangements for the Fijian national rugby trials last weekend in Lautoka. Our best players get flown everywhere and stay in top hotels, but ponder these arrangements for Fiji tour hopefuls on their way to their trials.

The trialists from Suva and three outlying villages had to be outside Rugby House in Suva on Saturday at 7am. The bus was to depart at 7.30am. If a player was not there it was assumed he would miss tour selection to Britain.

Along the way from Suva to Lautoka, which takes four hours at least, players from other villages were picked up by the bus. Last week's memo, issued by the Fiji RFU, ended with a reminder to all players to "please bring boots, socks and shorts (black or white)".

The bus was to arrive at Churchill Park, Lautoka, at 1pm and the game was to kick off at 3pm.

2002

A man of wine and song

Now let's see, what baggage can I give you now on new NZRFU chairman Jock Hobbs, seeing as he used to be a touring television commentary companion? He and I broadcast together in 1995 and 1996 in South Africa and France.

I remember this: the night in Johannesburg that news came through that Jock had been elected by postal vote on to the New Zealand council he called together six or seven of us and produced bottles of Moet & Chandon champagne as a celebration. When we tried to return the favour Jock said: "No, I'm buying. This is my moment." And more of the good stuff arrived.

Then there was the night in Paris. While on a late-night cruise of the jazz quarter of that great city, Jock, who is hardly fluent in French, moved from bar to bar, trying to find at least one open, so that the patrons could benefit from his sparkling renditions of several of the world's great jazz standards. A great singer is our man Hobbs – not!

Joseph Romanos Collection

Jock Hobbs — connoisseur of fine wines and music lover.

But Jock does love his music. A couple of years ago he was so moved by the presence of Neil Diamond in our country that he was seen boarding a plane to fly from Wellington to Christchurch for a concert.

And get this: if you see our new chairman sitting back somewhere with eyes closed and tape across his ears, it's not because he hankers for the old days of taping his ears and returning to the rugby field. No — that's just Jock trying to keep his Walkman plugs in over his beautiful cauliflower ears.

2002

Kicking is overvalued

When Blair Feeney recently landed seven penalty goals to help Otago beat Wellington in an NPC game and was then hailed as a hero by the Otago media, it prompted me to think about the role of the penalty in rugby. Surely we should all be more irritated when games are won by massive amounts of points accumulated by penalty goals.

I remember feeling uneasy as a kid after the British Lions had scored four tries in a test in Dunedin in 1959, yet lost 18-17 to New Zealand's six penalty goals. There was the same feeling when Andrew Mehrtens kicked nine penalties in Auckland in 1999 on the way to the All Blacks' 34-15 win over Australia (they scored two tries to our one).

Rugby league has the answer. The value of their penalty goal is only two points, so in league penalties are useful only in ones and twos – tries are the thing. Can anyone recall when a critical game of league was won by a player landing seven, eight or nine penalties in a game?

Do we want our showpiece games stopped so often so we can all watch one man kick for goal?

2002

The charming Horse has gone

Joseph Romanos Collection

We buried a wonderful media colleague and friend this week in Wellington. Alex Veysey had a brilliantly fertile and inventive mind at the typewriter and he played a massive role in recording the history of rugby and its personalities.

My favourite of his many books was *Ebony and Ivory*, which told with great humour the lives of those two ebullient characters, Stu Wilson and Bernie Fraser. It is still worth reading as an example of how a wonderful wordsmith can turn spoken humour into equally funny prose. His most famous work, titled simply *Colin Meads – All Black*, set the benchmark for All Black biographies. It is said to have sold 60,000 copies.

How prolific rugby writer Alex Veysey captured so brilliantly in book form the zany humour of All Black wingers Bernie Fraser *(left)* and Stu Wilson is beyond me.

It is also not widely known that Alex was very adept at the microphone as well. Indeed, he was probably New Zealand's first sports radio talkback host. In the late 1960s he would come into 2ZB in Wellington late on a Saturday afternoon and take an hour of calls about sports issues of the day.

Always charming, Alex had a slight problem remembering people's names. So he resorted to calling everyone in his wide circle of friends "Horse". It was almost a case of you knew you had made it as a friend if he greeted you that way. In turn he became "Horse" Veysey to his many friends.

2002

Dismissed, not retired hurt

A top international player who retired last week had a strong connection with New Zealand.

Springbok flanker Andre Venter (66 test caps) was a tough man, but met his match at Eden Park in 1997. In a Tri Nations test, referee Derek Bevan of Wales thought big Andre had lashed out at Sean Fitzpatrick's head. So out came the red card.

Venter, however, did not immediately head to the grandstand. Instead he stepped off the grass and sat down. And all the commentators thought the poor bloke had been hurt.

2002

Let the mad horse loose

All Black coach John Mitchell has not been the only one dishing out strange quotes or making great headlines for the media these past few weeks.

How's this from French rugby manager Jo Maso, when talking about his diminutive winger Vincent Clerc: "He will throw himself into Lomu as a mad horse does to a sequoia tree."

Or the South African newspaper *Die Afrikaans'* headline after the Springboks lost to Scotland. Across the front page the three words to describe the test match loss were: "Vrot, Vrotter, Vrotster", meaning Rotten, Rottener, Rottenest.

Welshman Scott Quinnell, when reflecting on his career, said that the most memorable quote he gave about rugby was picked up by the referee's microphone. It was when he told his Llanelli team-mates: "Okay boys, you heard what Didier Mene just said... 'attendez' means f******g wait!"

And this gem from Tana Umaga, after the All Blacks played most of their test against France having had three yellow cards handed out against them: "Now some of these guys will know what it's like to be a Hurricane and always play with 14 men."

2002

We won, let's eat

The Welsh are great ones for having dinners to celebrate their victories over the All Blacks. The 1953 Cardiff and Wales teams celebrated with one dinner per year for more than 50 years after they beat Bob Stuart's team.

And several years ago the Llanelli team that beat New Zealand 9-3 in 1972 had a big bash to celebrate 30 years since their club's finest victory.

A Welsh friend tells me the Llanelli dinner was a great show, with the captain of the Llanelli team, Delme Thomas, giving a powerful speech of remembrance and the emotional but delightful Ray Gravell bursting into tears all over again. Thank goodness Andy Hill, the man who kicked one of the dramatic penalty goals to clinch the win, lightened things with a story he swore was true.

Andy said: "Late that night after the win a young woman came up to me and offered to make love to me for a pound in bed, or a shilling in a rocking chair. I said I'd rather take the shilling option in the rocking chair. But in the end it cost me thirty quid because we wrecked the rocking chair!"

2002

Dead in his seat

Now here is a story about Llanelli that *is* true – I know because Earle Kirton and I saw it happen from our commentary box.

During the bleak, cold and miserable day in 1989 when the All Blacks played Llanelli, one of the new grandstands couldn't be opened for spectators because of dangerous winds. So more people than usual were packed into the old stand. Apparently, in the excitement of the second half, an old bloke died in his seat, just sitting squashed between other folks. Nobody noticed till the end of the game.

When it was discovered he had passed away, an old door was brought from somewhere into the stand. His friends gently raised the dead man on to the door. I well recall him being carried out of the ground, shoulder high, with a Llanelli scarf pressed into his hands, being cheered to the skies, and followed by hundreds of cheering bystanders.

Ladies? What ladies?

Peter Bush always had an eye for a great shot. Ian Kirkpatrick's 1972-73 All Blacks changed in some interesting places on their North American and European tour. Behind Kirkpatrick are Bob Burgess, Peter Whiting and Jeff Matheson *(right)*.

It won't last

Things we old-timers used to laugh at and say:

- "Yes, but this fad won't last long."

- Backs who wore headgear.

- Players who wore gloves.

- Players who wore shoulder-pads.

- Soccer-style jerseys with no collars.

- Players who had long hair.

- Commercial paint signs within the field of play.

- Tape strapping above the knees.

- Microphones on referees.

- Goal-kicking tees brought on the field by kids in mini-cars.

- Silly people in the grandstands leering at themselves when they know they're on television.

2001

Caught short

From this month's copy of *USA Rugby Magazine* comes this profile of the American women's international player Ellie Karvoski. Under the heading "Most Embarrassing Moment in Rugby", Ellie owns up: "It was in a practice match in Germany. I was running past the German sideline and got my shorts pulled down. I was not wearing the most appropriate undergarment for that game."

2003

To do before you die

The *Sydney Daily Telegraph* recently ran a column declaring "The 50 Things You Must Do Before You Die". The list included visiting the Taj Mahal, seeing Big Ben in London, doing a bungee jump, and so on. It got me thinking about something similar for the great game.

Why not a rugby list of 20, which might go something like this:

1. Attend a rugby dinner to listen to and admire a speech by Colin Meads.
2. Attend a rugby dinner to listen to and admire a speech by Eric Rush.
3. Travel with your home provincial team to support their Ranfurly Shield challenge.
4. Have your picture taken alongside the Ranfurly Shield.
5. Attend the Wellington international sevens tournament.
6a. If you are a rural person, watch an urban club game, then go home and talk about the difference.
6b. If you are an urban person, watch a rural club game, then go home and talk about the difference.
7. Ring a radio talkback announcer and break the mould by saying something *good* about New Zealand rugby.
8. Try to have a beer and listen to – but don't interrupt too often – any former All Black telling stories of being away on tour.
9. Read and understand the rugby law book.
10. Next time it comes around, go and see *Foreskin's Lament*.
11. Visit the New Zealand Rugby Museum in Palmerston North.
12. Return to your original rugby clubrooms and savour the memories.
13. Read either or both of Sir Terry McLean's best two books – *Willie Away* and *New Zealand Rugby Legends*.
14. Read and keep on a coffee table at home Ron Palenski's *Century in Black*.
15. Recall where you were when Colin Meads was sent off, or when Jonah Lomu scored his four tries against England, or when the All Blacks won the 1987 World Cup.

16. Buy a sensible pair of gumboots, so you can stand on the sideline in mud and support one of your kids, or a relative's or friend's kids, as they play Saturday morning rugby.

17. Admit that you're never too old to sample the hotdogs or pies at any rugby ground you go to.

18. Even if your financial situation is precarious, save like hell to make sure that one year you definitely get to the Hong Kong sevens.

19. Save your strongest shouting, and direct it at home towards TV commentators by all means, but never at referees at the grounds.

20. Condemn all those silly bastards who streak at games, because they interrupt your enjoyment of watching the rugby action.

2003

Selective recall

On the occasion of the England prop Jason Leonard reaching 100 tests for his country, the London *Evening Standard* asked Leonard to recall a highlight from each of those games. Some of the comments are quite startling to New Zealand readers.

Leonard says his memory of his second test, v Argentina in 1990, is: "[the England team] followed the New Zealand Maori team from hotel to hotel and at one there weren't any televisions. The Maoris had thrown them all out of the windows after losing and the hotel wasn't taking any chances with us."

Such a remark is interesting, because Leonard must have been referring to the 1988 New Zealand Maori team, which toured Argentina *two years* earlier. According to my trusty *New Zealand Rugby Almanack*, the Maori team played two games in that country, and won them both.

Leonard also claims that Sean Fitzpatrick made a racist remark about Nigerian-born Victor Ubogu during the England-New Zealand game at Twickenham in 1993. Leonard says it was surprising, because "one of Fitzy's props was Olo Brown and he's as Maori [sic] as they come".

2002

Four stars

Congratulations to St Bernard's College in Lower Hutt. This fine rugby establishment has no fewer than four former pupils playing in this year's World Cup. But none of the four will play for the All Blacks.

Earl Va'a and Dominic Feaunati are to play for Samoa and Inoke Afeaki and his brother Stanley for Tonga.

2003

Favourite food

I was having a word with All Black No 8 Jerry Collins one time. We got to talking about how far he's come in his young life. From being a knockabout four-year-old in a Samoan family that arrived in New Zealand, he was now about to strut his powerful presence in front of millions of people via worldwide television coverage of All Black matches.

Jerry says: "I can remember when we came here from Samoa and settled in Porirua as a family – we had to eat on the floor. Not only that, but we had no dinner set to eat with. My sister and I we shared one plate between us. That's all we had. And mum cooked us rice, spaghetti and corned beef. We loved it so much we used to ask for it for breakfast, lunch and dinner. The nutritionists around the All Blacks will probably be horrified, but that is still my favourite dish."

In 2006, Jerry became the first Samoan-born player to captain the All Blacks. H F Boy, of Lower Hutt, noted that Jerry was only the third test captain – of 61 so far – born off-shore. Dave Gallaher, an All Black from 1903-06, was born in Ireland and Cliff Porter, the 1923-30 All Black, was born in Scotland.

Jerry Collins — a spaghetti and corned beef man.

Cheering times

For such a long tournament as the 2007 World Cup, you will need to carefully protect your throat, so that you can be cheering as loudly at the end of seven weeks as at the start. Here are my suggestions of when to shout your loudest:

- For the first sight of the All Black team coming on to the field at any match.

- At the end of the haka.

- At the blast of the ref's whistle to start any All Black game.

- At the awarding of any scrum put-ins to New Zealand inside the opposition 22.

- At the scoring of any try by New Zealand

- For any successful sideline conversion by New Zealand.

- For any opposition shot at goal that misses from in front of the goalposts.

- When Richie McCaw is injured but gets up, shrugs and plays on.

- When Daniel Carter goes for the outside break and gets through.

- When the final whistle goes and another win has been posted by the All Blacks.

Fitting tribute

Congratulations to the organisers of the dinner in New Plymouth the other night, which paid tribute to the rugby career of great Taranaki man Andy Slater. There were 250 people packed into the appropriately named Legends Lounge at Yarrow Stadium to hear person after person pay their compliments to the man who played 182 games in the famous amber and black colours.

Special reference was made to the win by Taranaki over Auckland at Eden Park in 1996, when the Ranfurly Shield was at stake. Andy Slater was the captain that day and a whole swag of his team-mates honoured him at the function. They included the man who scored three tries for Taranaki that day, Dean Magon.

At the *This is Your Life*-style function there were many highlights, including video from Britain of some old Taranaki mates, Campbell Feather and Scott Lines. Todd Blackadder, currently living in Scotland, also featured with some video reminiscences.

But the highlight was when MC Phil Quinney introduced a "special star guest" to the crowd. The crowd hushed, and out came none other than… the hallowed Ranfurly Shield itself!

The Log o' Wood had been loaned by the Canterbury Rugby Union as its mark of respect for the 13 seasons of effort Andy Slater had given to his province. What a climax to a great night it was.

2003

The fullback poser

In 2003, the programme for the Wales-England international became a collector's item. According to Eddie Butler, the BBC television commentator, New Zealander Steve Hansen, who was then the Welsh coach, listed three fullbacks in his playing XV.

In his commentary Butler said: "Kevin Morgan was published as centre fullback, Gareth Thomas was listed left fullback and Rhys Williams was called right fullback."

The new terminology continued, with Hansen recalling David Humphreys to his team, and naming him as the captain of the on-field Welsh playing XV. But Colin Charvis, who had been leader on the field in the previous match against Italy, was not dropped from the leadership entirely. Instead, for the England game, Charvis was renamed "Welsh squad captain".

Confused? You should be. Mind you, rugby's version of being politically correct has extended to Australia too. The Brumbies listed three vice-captains for their team in the 2003 season.

Seeing red

You think we've had it bad with red cards and rough play in New Zealand rugby lately? Well, cop this story from one recent French club game, between Tarbes and Tyrosse. Referee Eric Gauzins, fed up with all the squabbling, scrabbling, stamping and stomping, took action. Blowing his whistle hard all afternoon, Monsieur Gauzins brandished no fewer than five red cards and seven yellow cards.

Players from both teams left and returned at a high rate of knots. At one point there were only 12 players from each side on the field.

Tarbes were the home side and won 44-6, but four of the five red cards were dished out against their players. Even one of their halfback replacements, who was on the field for only a few minutes, was returned to the sideline, having seen red as well.

2003

Total integration

Well done to the cast and crew of the epic *The Last Samurai*, which was filmed over several months in Taranaki. The film people really integrated well into local society. Not only did the *Sunday Star-Times* print a shot of the star, Tom Cruise, coming out of a local fish and chip shop, but the cast has had several very strong connections with rugby in the region.

For example, in the Taranaki Dewer Shield sevens competition, which traditionally kicks off each year's club play, *The Last Samurai* entered a team, made up of a mix of New Zealand and Japanese players from the crew. The team, one of 21 in the tournament, competed vigorously, though without major success.

Tom Cruise — sevens rugby player?

Several days later, filming moved to Pukekura Park, in New Plymouth, for an English garden party scene. For that sequence the venerable New Plymouth sportsground was transformed into an old-style British parade ground. There was to be a grand march of Samurai warriors past esteemed English gentlemen and their good ladies. Many extras were needed from around New Plymouth.

One of the most notable of the extras standing in the crowd, and no doubt looking appropriately noble and dignified, was the former All Black and All Black coach Peter Burke.

2004

Aviation ace

Congratulations to Peter Clark, a veteran television freelance soundman from many a rugby telecast over the last 30 years. Last week you might have read the story about an Air New Zealand flight from Napier to Auckland, on which the captain, Gary Parata, took ill.

Peter, who had worked the Hurricanes-Bulls game, was a passenger on the plane. He offered to help, because he "had had a lot to do with aviation". His offer was accepted and he sat in with the First Officer, Kim Cadwallader, and read gauges and checklists as the plane landed safely.

Some of the passengers did not even notice that Captain Parata had rested at the back of the plane during the flight.

Peter's dedication to obtaining correct sound from our television sports events is on a par with his love and commitment to aviation matters.

2003

Haunted by tiddlywinks

Remember Tana Umaga's funny quip, which we all heard via the television microphones, during the Hurricanes-Crusaders semi-final the other week in Christchurch?

Tana protested to referee Peter Marshall about his control of the game, saying: "This is not tiddlywinks we're playing, Peter."

At the All Blacks announcement the other day I complimented Tana on introducing that new word to rugby commentary.

"Yes, but it's already come back to haunt me," he said. "I played 20 minutes last Saturday for Petone against Old Boys-University and at one point I went into the tackle ball area. I did everything perfectly, I thought, but I got penalised. I stood up to complain to the ref, but I was cut short by a deep voice from the other team. The voice said: 'Come on Tana, back you go, this isn't tiddlywinks we're playing here!'"

2003

Tana Umaga — anyone for tiddlywinks?

Young leaders

Being made captain of England at the age of just 23 in 2004 was a great honour for Jonny Wilkinson. At the time of his appointment much was made about having a major test team captained by someone so young. However, Wilkinson is far from the youngest to lead his country.

Here's my list of "baby" test captains:

19 years 8 months – Fred Stokes, England, 1871
20 years 7 months – Gareth Edwards, Wales, 1967
20 years 9 months – Lisandro Arbizu, Argentina, 1992
21 years 2 months – Trevor Allan, Australia, 1947
21 years 3 months – Herb Lilburne, New Zealand, 1929
21 years 11 months – Ken Catchpole, Australia, 1961
21 years 11 months – Rene Crabos, France, 1921
22 years 11 months – Will Carling, England, 1988

World's worst

John Scott, the England No 8 of the 1980s, has been claiming quite proudly that he might have been the world's worst test captain. Scott, who always lived in Cardiff but was English by birth, points out that he led his country in four tests and lost them all.

That got me thinking about New Zealand rugby captains. I've heard, more than once, well-known hard case Stu Wilson decry his record as an All Black test skipper. Not everyone recalls that Stu took the All Blacks to Britain on the short tour in 1983. There, his team had a loss against England and a draw against Scotland.

However, Stu can rest easy. The great Sean Fitzpatrick was an All Black test captain during 10 losses. But let's be fair – Fitzy also happened to lead the All Blacks to 41 test victories.

2004

Hair's to Grahame Thorne

Keith Quinn Collection

The look that caused such a sensation in 1983. Grahame Thorne shocked the nation when he decided to go the curly way. Back then, it wasn't quite in the traditional All Black image.

The winning ball

Buenos Aires correspondent and good friend Frankie Deges has provided this priceless piece of rugby trivia from the World Cup final at Auckland in 1987.

Frankie writes: "In years gone by when the final whistle blew many of the players in the major games would try to grab the ball, which would later become a wonderful memento of their test career. If any of the players in the 1987 final in Auckland wanted the ball they would have had to wrestle it from a man from Cordoba, Argentina, named Elmo Bursa.

"Elmo explains: 'My club was on tour in New Zealand and we got tickets to the final. In the last moments of the game, when New Zealand was winning, I saw the proud French come back, with Pierre Berbizier touching down under the posts. An easy goal from Didier Camberabero followed. Someone tried to grab the ball, but it bounced away and fell into my arms. A Kiwi guy next to me tried to take it. I was about to throw it back when referee Kerry Fitzgerald blew for fulltime. The ball is now proudly at my Cordoba Athletic club.'"

The way it was

A special thanks to an old friend, Mike Whatman, of Lower Hutt, who has found a long lost scrapbook of one of the forgotten All Black tours of Australia. Mike has kindly sent it to me for safekeeping.

The scrapbook is of the 1951 All Black team, which was captained by Otago's Peter Johnstone. The team played 12 games and won the lot, bringing home the Bledisloe Cup after Australia had won it in 1949.

A number of the team's travel arrangements have caught my eye. For example, the team travelled by flying boat to and from New Zealand. On their return to Auckland they played against Auckland only hours after touching down. The All Blacks won 9-3 but some reports said the team looked "quite jaded". Well, who wouldn't be after flying all night strapped, sitting upright, in the bouncing, thunderous flying boats?

Reading through the clippings there was one early hint of the world of professional rugby that was to follow nearly half a century later. While the Auckland players were presented with travelling rugs (whatever they were) on departure, and while Bob Duff, of Canterbury, was given a shaving kit, the dastardly Central Otago Rugby Union knew the way the rugby world was heading and presented its centre, Tommy Lynch, with a wallet.

2004

No place for the faint-hearted

Three examples here that there might be more going on in those rucks than we can see from the grandstand.

In *A Life Worth Living*, a biography of great Wallaby prop Sir Nicholas Shehadie, Nick reckons that years ago he was caught in the bottom of a ruck when Randwick played Eastwood in a club game. His face finished squashed against that of his old Wallaby touring buddy, prop Doug Keller. As bodies tumbled all around them, Keller announced to Nick that his wife had, just that morning, given birth to twin sons. The two men embraced in joy and then continued the game in opposition to each other.

That reminds me of a similar Stu Wilson story. Stu, who never, ever, liked rucks, was once caught at the bottom of one in a game between Wellington and Southland. Under the tangle of limbs and legs, a horrible Southland face, with broken teeth and a smashed nose, was suddenly pressed against Stu's impeccably groomed visage. Stu looked up in horror and, hoping to distract the opponent from possibly eating him, said: "G'day mate, got the time?"

And one more from the memory banks. Gareth Edwards reckons that in his test debut, for Wales against the All Blacks at Cardiff in 1967, he was mighty fearful as he dived for a skidding loose ball and the crunching, thumping All Black forwards rushed for it as well.

Edwards reckons that Wellington loose forward Graham Williams was first to go over the top. He landed on his knees and formed a kind of "body block". Edwards maintains to this day that Williams said: "Crawl under here son, and you'll be all right." Edwards did, and lived. I asked Graham Williams about this a few years ago, and he remembers the incident well.

2004

Gisborne misses out

It was a shame the All Blacks didn't make it to Gisborne for their planned week-long training session, because Gisborne is one of the towns in New Zealand where the All Blacks have never played a game.

Had the weather been fine they wouldn't have played one there this time either, but it does raise the question: how many New Zealand towns have the All Blacks played official games in?

This is my list: Albany, Ashburton, Auckland, Blenheim, Carterton, Christchurch, Dunedin, Greymouth, Hamilton, Invercargill, Masterton, Napier, Oamaru, Palmerston North, Pukekohe, Rotorua, Timaru, Wanganui, Wellington, Whangarei.

I haven't listed Levin, where in the 1970s there was a pre-season, non-first-class match played.

2003

The wit of Will

A bit of a lad is England centre Will Greenwood. After a match in 2003 he was quoted as saying: "If several instances in the game had gone our way things would have been different. Mind you, if my grandma had had balls she'd have been my granddad."

A little uncouth, I'd have thought, but maybe it's just Greenwood's way of talking. Once, when discussing which part of England he came from, he said: "I'm a northern monkey, born in Blackburn, brought up on a staple diet of football, rugby league and bingo in the village hall. For us a trip to the local chippy was a night out."

Greenwood maintained that outspoken tradition in his 2004 book *Will: The Autobiography of Will Greenwood*. Few New Zealanders will be rushing to buy it. Of the experience of being in New Zealand in 2003, he writes: "There is little point in reading the newspapers if you are an Englishman in New Zealand to play a rugby match. The news is always the same: England are rubbish and arrogant; New Zealand are simply marvellous and lovely guys with it. But even if you manage to avoid the crap they write, you cannot get away from the impression that there is not a soul in the country who would stop to pee on you if you were on fire."

Tight fit for legendary locks

Three of the greatest locks in rugby history: Colin Meads (*left*), Frik du Preez and Willie John McBride. Judging by the fit of their suits, they'd be more comfortable in rugby kit.

Are you awake?

This Irish story comes from a recent column by John Eales.

Apparently the former Wallaby captain, these days a businessman and lower-grade club basketball player, had just arrived in Dublin and, being quite tired, went straight to bed. Before turning out the light in his hotel room he arranged for a wake-up call for the next morning.

Eales takes up the story: "Next morning I woke somewhat earlier and went down to breakfast, during which there was an announcement that I had a telephone call at reception. There, I was handed the receiver and the operator said, 'Good morning Mr Eales, this is your 8am wake-up call'."

2004

Worst for the Welsh

When your country's rugby fortunes are haemorrhaging, as Wales' seem to be these days, then you can expect bad things from the media.

Graham Clutton, writing in London's *Daily Telegraph*, listed "the six worst moments in Welsh rugby history" as:

1. 1991 – losing 63-6 to Australia in Brisbane, then the Welsh players brawling among themselves in the Ballymore clubhouse.
2. 1994 – losing 26-24 to Canada in Cardiff, Canada's most significant win over a leading IRB country.
3. 1998 – losing 96-13 to South Africa in Pretoria, the biggest defeat ever.
4. 2001 – the Bridgend club informing its members that because of mounting debts the club might close in one week.
5. 2002 – Graham Henry resigns from the position of national coach.
6. 2002 – consultant Robin Allen is brought in to the Welsh Rugby Union on a £1000-a-day fee to stabilise the financial crisis in the union.

Some strange calls there, wouldn't you say? No mention by Mr Clutton of the 50-year gap since Wales last beat the All Blacks, or the *average* score of 45 points per game that Wales have conceded to New Zealand over the last eight test matches, spanning 16 years. Or Wales losing 16-13 to Western Samoa in Cardiff at the 1991 Rugby World Cup.

2003

Let them sing

It's no wonder rugby standards are dropping all over Wales. For last weekend's Wales-France match, Welsh fans travelling by train to Paris were formally advised beforehand that they could face jail if they were caught singing on the train.

It's true! One of the train companies, Arriva Trains Wales, has introduced a bylaw that bans singing "without advance written permission" from the train operator. The law states: "No person on the railway shall, to the annoyance of any other person, sing."

2004

Idi Amin and rugby

The world is a better place now that Idi Amin Dada has died. However, the huge, ruthless former Uganda dictator was once a sportsman of significance. He was heavyweight boxing champion of Uganda from 1951-60 and, as a member of the British army based in Uganda, was also a feared rugby player.

According to the London *Daily Telegraph's* obituary, he was 6ft 6in tall and weighed 18st. He was a reserve for the East Africa XV that lost 39-12 to the 1955 British Lions.

This month's *African Insights* newsletter reported: "In rugby Amin was an animal. His British officers would take a hammer to his forehead and prime him for his rugby contests. That would release his mean streak and competitive spirit. Off he would then go to destroy the opposition."

2003

At last, a chance for a dram

We take some things for granted in New Zealand. Fans at our major grounds have long been able to enjoy alcoholic drinks while watching rugby. With only the odd exception, we have been comfortable with this arrangement and behaved accordingly.

On the other hand, the Scottish Rugby Union and local Scottish licensing authorities have been so paranoid about alcohol at sports grounds that none has been allowed inside the famous rugby shrine of Murrayfield in Edinburgh. Until this coming weekend, that is.

For the upcoming Scottish Club Cup finals day a special marquee and stall will be set up to allow fans to take a drink if they wish to.

This is a major change from the time I was taken on a tour of the "new" Murrayfield ground and shown the elaborate camera security system. The lenses were so powerful that each camera could identify who was sitting in each seat in the stadium and what their hands were doing. Such cameras made it all the more difficult for a Scotsman to take a dram from his hip flask secreted in his sporran.

2004

Little help for the minnows

Here, courtesy of Fijian magazine *Teivovo*, and its editor, Jeremy Duxbury, is your background for arguing about whether the world's major rugby nations have helped the rugby minnows of the South Pacific:

Australia last played in Fiji in 1984, and have never played in Tonga or Samoa.

New Zealand have never played a test in Fiji, Samoa or Tonga.

South Africa have never played a test in Fiji, Samoa or Tonga.

Argentina have never played a test in Fiji, Samoa or Tonga.

Only once in 90 years have Fiji played South Africa (in South Africa in 1996).

Only once have Tonga played South Africa (in South Africa in 1997).

Outside the World Cup, England have never played Tonga.

Outside the World Cup England have played only two matches against Samoa (in 1995 and 2005).

Outside the World Cup, Scotland have played just one match against Tonga (in 2001).

The British Lions have played only one game in the Pacific (against Fiji in 1977).

That leaves Wales, France, Scotland, Italy and Ireland as the major nations who have turned up in the islands for at least one full international. New Zealand did make something of a breakthrough with the Junior All Blacks playing in Samoa, Tonga and Fiji in 2007.

2007

Catcalls from the ages

I always enjoy good catcalls from rugby crowds, especially when they boom out with clarion-like simplicity in quiet moments. The warmth of response from those sitting nearby is fun to be part of.

The *Sydney Morning Herald* reported the other day that during the recent Australia-England game, when Charlie Hodgson was lining up a kick at goal, a couple of lads sitting near the touchline started chanting "Jonny'd get it, Jonny'd get it!" Their cry gradually gained volume and momentum and, not surprisingly, Hodgson then missed the rather comfortable shot at goal.

The crowd then roared with further delight when Charlie looked daggers in the direction of the chant.

It reminded me of the times that crowds at Athletic Park used to try to put off Auckland players: "Hey Kirwan, your mother wore army boots!" was a good call. Or, "Hey Fox, your mother swam after troop ships!"

The only trouble with those excellent efforts by the Wellington crowds was that John Kirwan invariably scored a try, and that damn Grant Fox kicked every goal in sight.

2004

Crabs are alive

A note to members of the New Zealand sevens squad who visited Shanghai in 2001. I'm sure that team members will be very relieved to know that the Hairy Crabs Rugby Football Club is still going strong. On June 13, as part of the curtain-raisers to the China-Singapore test, the club is fielding not one, but two teams.

According to the flyer sent to me by the China Rugby Union, the Hairy Crabs Black team are playing HMS Exeter XV at 10.30am, followed by the Hairy Crabs Green team against the Shanghai Sports Institute. Those games will be followed by the World Cup qualifier at 2.30pm.

For those who missed the visit to beautiful Shanghai in 2001, a Hairy Crab is a rather delightful little seafood delicacy, best served fried lightly, with a touch of chilly sauce added. The name means nothing more, you understand. It is just a name that the ex-pat rugby players of Shanghai thought would fit aptly on a rugby team's letterhead.

2004

The Olympic All Black

Ever wonder about the All Blacks and the Olympic Games? New Zealand never competed at rugby at the Olympics, but did you know that we have an "Olympic All Black" in our rugby history?

Selwyn George Bremner is Wellington-based these days but in the 1950s he played for Auckland, Wellington, Manawatu and Canterbury. Known always as "Mick" Bremner, his "Olympic All Black" tag is slightly misleading. It came from the fact that Mick was chosen for the All Blacks only in Olympic Games years.

In 1952, when the games were held in Helsinki, Mick was an Auckland rep and was picked to play the Wallabies in the second test in Wellington. He then had to wait until 1956, when the Olympics were staged in Melbourne, to be picked again. He played one test, against South Africa.

The third and final outing for the sturdy second five-eighths was on the All Black tour of South Africa in 1960 – Rome was the Olympic venue that year. Mick was elevated to the vice-captaincy and did sterling midweek service for the Wilson Whineray-led team.

2006

Memories of Morrie

Morrie Dixon was a real character, a good New Zealand rugby man from the 1950s.

Morrie was a winger par excellence, a Canterbury battler on the field, an All Black, a representative and South Island selector, a publican later in life and a superb raconteur about the good old days.

He once recounted to me how he had been a 10-year-old tap-dancer in a show-business ensemble on a ship heading into Sydney Harbour when he was told World War II had broken out.

Two noted New Zealand rugby writers recently told other good Dixon stories.

Ron Palenski emailed from Dunedin: "Morrie was a really good bloke. There's a story about him playing in the South African test in Dunedin in 1956. Mark Irwin went off with a serious leg injury and lock forward Stan

"Tiny" Hill figured he'd be fingered to go into the front row [There were no replacements in those days]. So Hill decided to make himself invisible – as much as he could – and took off across the field and was out on the wing next to Dixon when the captain Bob Duff started looking around. Dixon yelled out: "He's over here Bob, Tiny's over here!" Hill's response to Morrie was: "Thanks, you bastard."

And Phil Gifford's story in the *Sunday Star-Times* is worth re-telling too: "[One great rugby rivalry] was revived by Morrie Dixon's death. His provincial nemesis was the All Black left wing from Wellington, Ron Jarden.

"Once, in the tunnel at Lancaster Park, Dixon said to Jarden, 'It's your lucky day Ron'. There was not a word from Jarden. 'Definitely your lucky day,' repeated Dixon. More silence from Jarden. 'Very, very lucky,' chirped Dixon. Jarden finally cracked. 'What do you mean?' Dixon smiled innocently and said, 'Because they've got the stretcher on your side of the field today'."

2004

Respect for the tie

Thanks go to John Brodie, a New Zealander who has lived in Brisbane for more than 30 years. John emailed to concur with the story that even if you are presented with an All Black tie it is usually the case that you do not "qualify" to wear it unless you have been chosen to play for our famous team.

John said that over the years as a liaison officer for touring teams into Brisbane he had had four All Blacks ties presented to him. But he said he had never worn one. He went further to say that one time Buck Shelford presented him with his All Black jersey after a test at Ballymore.

"Unlike my collection of jerseys from other countries, I've never brought myself to put it on," he said. "Visiting Kiwi friends and their children have loved having their photo with it on. But not me."

2004

Wairoa – Ranfurly Shield country

Keith Quinn Collection

The famous 1922 Wairoa sub-union team, who held the Ranfurly Shield, if only for a few moments. Hawke's Bay were the Ranfurly Shield-holders through the early 1920s and the prized Ranfurly Shield was kept in safe keeping in Napier.

However, when Napier sub-union played their neighbours, Wairoa sub-union, in 1922, they took the shield along for the day. It was carried by horse-drawn carriage and shown off along the way.

Wairoa, who were not of first-class status, pulled off a surprise win over their Napier rivals, and as a reward were allowed to have their photograph taken with the famous trophy. To this day, the photo, much enlarged, can be found hanging in the Wairoa Athletic Club, the symbol of a prized Wairoa legend.

Peppers will stop the rain

Memo to all rugby ground-staff throughout New Zealand: here is one cure for sodden and muddy grounds that you might not have heard about. At the National Sports Stadium in Singapore, in the lead-up to the IRB Singapore sevens tournament, there were daily heavy mid-afternoon rain-storms.

Undeterred, on the morning of the first day of the tournament, the head groundsman at the stadium was seen chopping up a liberal pile of green chilli peppers. He carried them on to the rugby field and scattered them over the grass. The groundsman told a curious television film crew that if he remembered to do it, the chilli peppers would keep away the rainstorms.

Sure enough, the normal sequence of heavy showers did not happen that day.

On day two, however, we have to assume the groundsman either slept in, or there was a citywide shortage of chilli peppers. It hosed down most of the afternoon.

2004

Farewell to the doyen

Last Sunday morning the phone at my place shrilled with one of those calls a little too early to be about regular family stuff. The caller was Jock McLean, from Auckland. He was ringing to say that his dad, the great rugby and sports writer, Sir Terry McLean, had passed away overnight.

Jock told me that his dad, only a few days off 91, had watched the All Blacks play the Pacific Islanders. He had complained of a headache, which might have been caused by the narrow winning margin of New Zealand. Hours later he slipped away.

To die so soon after viewing a test was an appropriate way for "the doyen" to go. Quite simply, there will never be another Terry ("T P") McLean. Andy Haden once described him as "the white pointer shark" of rugby reporting, and that was true up to a point. From his first writings about the game, in 1930, when he joined the *Hawke's Bay Sun*, and later in

The one and only Terry McLean.

millions of words in his books and for the *New Zealand Herald*, he could be a gnarly old bugger.

But T P was a man of great worldliness and warmth and that made his written praise, which came plentifully many times, all the greater for those in receipt of it. Would that we had writing like his today.

I toured with T P many times in the 1970s and 1980s. He was a unique character. He was always impeccably dressed, wearing a tie carefully chosen to match the occasion, and he usually covered his bald head with a well-worn cheese-cutter hat. He had a unique way of working. In the days long before lightweight laptops, he carried to grounds a heavy portable typewriter, into which he would roll his pages of paper and quite simply thunder away.

It was not his style to go searching for after-match quotes from captains or coaches. T P used to say: "*The New Zealand Herald* sent me to this test, therefore they want *my* opinions." So he gave them his best, often working deep into the night and early morning.

There is a story, perhaps apocryphal, that he once worked all night to make a deadline and greeted a colleague at his hotel door at breakfast time in his pyjamas with QWERTYUIOP written in reverse across his forehead!

In recent years T P's physical health was not great, but to visit and chat with him at his Auckland rest home was still challenging. He was always very alert to what was happening in rugby. His phone calls went straight to the topic of the day. There was scant time for introductions about the weather and the like. Usually it was: "Quinn my boy, what *are* they up to in the Rugby Union *now*!"

I have many favourite T P McLean stories – the man was a classic, and the 29 books he wrote are testament to his commitment to the game.

His story about trying to find the sent-home, self-exiled 1972 All Black Keith Murdoch in the wilds of Western Australia was McLean at his best. While the other reporters on tour knew nothing of Murdoch's whereabouts, T P flew from Perth in a Fokker Friendship to the town of Newman and then by chartered plane to Port Hedland.

There he confronted Murdoch in a Cowra work camp. Let me go now to a summary of part of McLean's writing of the meeting between the two in the *New Zealand Herald*: "It would be absurd to describe our meeting, far out in the wilderness, as containing the politeness implicit in Mr Stanley's 'Dr Livingstone I presume?'

"As I moved towards Murdoch his eyes turned steely, and he gestured with a thumb. 'Back in the bus,' he said curtly, 'just keep moving.'

"As I offered some greeting he jerked his thumb again. 'Back in the bus,' he said again. 'I have nothing to say to you now, or at any time. I have read what you have said about me. It's all lies.'

"'You haven't,' said I, 'surely read everything I have written about you, have you?'

"'Maybe not,' said Murdoch. 'But it's all bloody lies.' He then shouted to my driver: 'Who brought this "so and so" up here?'

"The 'so and so', if inaccurate as to gender, was a most offensive term. 'Get back on the bus,' said Murdoch again. 'Just keep moving…'"

One more thing about dear old T P. The great American sportswriter Red Smith was once asked: "Why write about sport?" Smith's reply captures for me what Sir Terence Power McLean offered to our country. Smith wrote: "Sport is not really a play world. I think it's the real world. The people in sport who we're writing about are living and loving and dying and trying to make their way in life, just as the politicians and the bricklayers are. The man who reports on their games therefore contributes his small bit to the record of his time."

To repeat: there'll never be another T P McLean.

2004

He's out

The T P McLean funeral in Auckland last week was a time for the trading of many a good story about a unique sports-writing character. I particularly liked the Peter Bush story, about the time in South Africa in 1976 when some of the New Zealand reporters were kicking a ball around on the sideline at an All Black practice session.

One of the players decided to put T P's prowess as a catcher to the test. A high ball came out of a clear blue South African sky. It hit T P on the head and down he went. As he was assisted to his feet he looked about and asked: "And which of those All Blacks was it who kicked that ball?" It had actually been Otago winger Neil Purvis. When told this, McLean, still feeling his sore head, said in his growliest tone: "Right! That boy will never again be mentioned in the *New Zealand Herald*."

2004

Full integration

I've had a follow-up from last week's story about the New Zealand women's rugby team playing in the main game in Vancouver while the New Zealand Maori team played the curtain-raiser.

Apparently this was not a first for rugby. At Murrayfield, in Scotland, last March, the top male players of Scotland and France did battle in a Six Nations game, and after they left the field and many of the crowd of 65,000 were heading home, out ran the top *women's* teams of those same two countries.

It was reported that the idea was a great success, with many staying to watch. The idea is part of the Scotland union's attempt at full integration of men and women's rugby.

It's surely far better than what happens here, where the New Zealand women's team, world champions and all that, usually play their biggest games as early curtain-raisers to big masculine events.

2004

One for the mantelpiece

A picture that Scottish winger Roger Baird might like to have on the mantelpiece. Baird played 27 tests for Scotland from 1981-88, but perhaps because of Scotland's conservative style, never scored a test try. This is his only test touchdown — for the British Lions against New Zealand, at Dunedin in 1983.

Who's kicking?

The French do things differently, don't they? National coach Bernard Laporte announced his team for their game last weekend against Wales. He included two backline players from the famous Toulouse club. They were Jean-Baptiste Elissalde and Frederic Michalak, the halfback and flyhalf. Both are brilliant runners and superb goal-kickers. "Who," asked reporters, "will do the goal-kicking?"

Laporte replied (and one can imagine him giving a Gallic shrug of the shoulders as he spoke): "It's for them to decide."

Them to decide! Imagine Graham Henry, the All Black coach, giving a similarly nonchalant Kiwi shrug of the shoulders and saying that when wondering who would be kicking for the All Blacks this year.

2004

The women rule

The New Zealand Maori team, travelling to North America for their Churchill Cup series, played a curtain-raiser game in Vancouver recently. They won their opening game 111-3 and then left the field.

The two teams for the main game then ran on. They were the New Zealand and Canadian *women's* teams. It was declared that out of deference to the full international standing of the Black Ferns, the New Zealand women's team, they would play as top-of-the-bill ahead of the non-international status of the male Maori team.

2004

A photo with meaning

Tears flowed for one young woman at the Peter Bush/Colin Meads charity auction night in Wellington last week. "Bushie" is offering 25 of his best rugby photos for auction in three cities this winter. The amount raised in Auckland and Wellington is approaching $100,000. Bidding was keen for each of the famous photos in Wellington.

It was when Rachel Taylor's bid of $750 secured lot 14 that the tears flowed. The photo showed Sid Going about to wrap up opposing halfback Gary Grey during the third test against Australia at Eden Park in 1972. New Zealand won the game 38-3.

Rachel was more concerned with the other man who was prominent in the dramatic pic. It was the referee – her late father, Alan Taylor, of Canterbury. That was the third and last test that Alan controlled in his fine career. The first was a strange one – he came on as a substitute for an injured Pat Murphy during a test at Lancaster Park in 1965. The likeable Alan died in his 40s after completing a history of Canterbury rugby referees.

2004

Millard memories

MILLARD STAND OPENING
AUCKLAND v WELLINGTON
June 23, 1962

RUGBY WEEKLY SOUVENIR 1/-

The Millard Stand was a grand old Athletic Park landmark.

Left: This is the programme from its opening day in 1962. The stand offered the best view in world rugby — well, we locals thought so, anyway. Such a shame we had to wear crampons to get to the top!

And *(below)* 37 years later the old stand came crashing down. All in the name of progress.

Our Feng Shui is all wrong

Want to know the real reasons why England, beaten by Ireland a couple of weeks back, are on a downward spiral at the moment? It's clearly not because Jonny Wilkinson is injured and Martin Johnson has retired. No, it's because they're being distracted by other matters.

For example, we know the World Cup-winning England team all got gongs from the Queen, the largesse extending to many of the 13 officials who travelled to Australia.

But now there is more evidence coming to light. When England played Scotland in February, Sir Clive Woodward reportedly complained about the Feng Shui being wrong in the Murrayfield dressing room.

The latest news is that aroma therapists and perfume experts are being called in to provide the right kind of soothing aromas in the England dressing room before tests. Apparently, having the right type of smells in a dressing room can affect people's moods.

It is my sure and definite prediction that if this policy of believing in exterior influences continues, England rugby will crash and burn permanently. What's wrong with the traditional smells of a rugby dressing room, with that beautiful mix of liniment odour, old mud-caked boots, last night's body odour from 20 men, the acrid smoke of the assistant coach's cigarettes, and of a flanker who visited an Indian restaurant 24 hours earlier, with disastrous consequences?

2004

No-frills Tony

Congratulations must go to Tony Woodcock, of the 2005 All Black forward pack. Tony wins the prize for taking the field for the recent test against Australia in Sydney without a bandage in sight. No knee-supports, no thigh "suitcase handles" (or whatever those lineout gripping assists are called), no ankle-wrappings, no wristbands, no elbow dressings and no headbands. Just plain old, clean-cut Tony. Even the recent Clark Gable pencil-thin moustache was gone.

2005

Waiapu pays tribute

Congratulations to the Waiapu Rugby Club on the beautiful East Coast. Last weekend the club honoured its most famous local with the opening of the George Nepia Memorial Park. The ground is situated in the little settlement of Rangitukia, and is over the road from the local marae.

In his heyday the great All Black played for the Rangitukia club. After George's passing many young people left the district and the club went defunct. It was reopened recently as Waiapu RFC and a great programme of events was set down for last Saturday.

Get this:

10.30am – formal dedication of the new ground.

11am – kids' tug-of-war contests, followed by Past v Present players game.

Midday – a hangi was lifted. "A real hangi, not one of those plastic ones you get in the cities," said club president John Manuel.

2pm – the clubrooms were open to everyone to enter and watch the Northland-Nelson Bays Division II play-off game.

"What about the Division I final game later that day?" I asked John. "Won't members be invited to stay and watch that one too?"

"No," said John, "the club is supposed to be closed by then. By early evening we reckon everybody should be home."

2004

A tough game for refs

This from American referee Fred Thomas in a recent issue of the United States *Rugby* magazine. Fred says his most embarrassing moment in rugby came "two minutes into a recent match in Omaha. I accidentally banged heads with one of the players, opening up a two-inch cut above one eye.

"A medic stopped the bleeding and with it taped I controlled the rest of the game. Then I went to the hospital to get it stitched up. The nurses gave me a hard time about participating in a sport where the ref gets sent to hospital."

2004

Eric will be missed

Peter Bush, the great photographer, and I have been lamenting the fact that we have not seen much in the way of newspaper tributes to that very fine All Black and Aucklander Eric Boggs who passed away recently.

Peter recalled being coached by Eric in an Auckland junior rep team in about 1948. He said: "We loved Eric. I remember in particular when we travelled down to Hamilton for a game, he made the bus pull over to the side of the road at Ngaruawahia, where he bought each of us in the squad a pie. In 1948 that must have been quite an expense."

According to Peter, Eric was rather superstitious. "I was taking pictures at Eden Park one time when Eric was playing for Auckland. Whenever the opposition goal-kicker was lining up a shot, Eric would grab the goalposts, shake them and call out 'rabbits'. And you know, sometimes Eric's curse on the kicker worked!"

2004

There was no Suzie

It was irritating to tune into Australia's Fox Sports TV news last Saturday morning and hear the station's reporter going on about "Suzie" being at work in Christchurch before the weekend's test against South Africa and causing a tummy bug in the All Black camp.

Earlier in the week the Planet-Rugby website ran a "Has Suzie snuck into Christchurch?" headline.

If ever there was a case of some people's fertile imagination becoming fact and folklore, then the Suzie story is it.

So let me repeat, once and for all-time: THERE NEVER WAS HARD EVIDENCE THAT A WOMAN NAMED SUZIE WORKED AT THE ALL BLACKS' HOTEL IN JOHANNESBURG DURING THE WORLD CUP IN 1995.

THERE WAS NEVER PROOF THAT ANYONE NAMED SUZIE CAUSED THE ALL BLACKS TO BE POISONED THAT FATEFUL WORLD CUP WEEK.

The All Blacks did suffer from food poisoning before the 1995 World Cup final. A violent stomach bug swept through many of the team. And the *bug* might have affected the team's play in the final. But no-one has ever produced Suzie, or her surname, or what she looked like, or her work records at the hotel, or where she lived, or where she disappeared to immediately after the test.

But it seems her spectre is still very real to some people. Why don't we just accept facts that we know? And they are that the Suzie story is, or was, just a figment of a few people's imagination.

2004

Rugby's Olympic connection

Keith Quinn Collection

No All Black has competed at the Olympics for New Zealand, though some have gone close. Mark Irwin, the 1950s prop, was a fine rower who went within a whisker of making the 1956 Olympic team. Other props Gary Knight and Steve McDowell might have won Olympic selection later for wrestling and judo respectively, and several All Black wingers, such as Peter Henderson, Tony Steel, Rod Heeps, Terry Morrison and Bruce Hunter, have won national running titles without earning Olympic selection.

However, here's one time when the Olympic movement and test rugby definitely intercepted. This is one of the earliest action photographs of any significant rugby union match. The two teams, Stade Français and Racing Club de Paris, are playing the first French club final, at the Bois de Boulogne, in 1892. Racing won 4-3.

The referee is none other than Baron Pierre de Coubertin, better remembered as the man who launched the modern Olympic Games. Incidentally, the following season the final was controlled by New Zealander, Thomas "Darby" Ryan.

Clive gets precious

The way Clive Woodward spoke after the Auckland test match wasn't his only brain-to-mouth misconnection. According to *The Australian*, while in New Zealand Sir Clive ("call me Clive") was interviewed by an English television crew and told millions of British viewers that "the upcoming test will be a massive clash and if we can dominate with our forwards and maximise our kicking game with Jonny Wilkinson, errrr…"

Then he stopped, realising that superstar Jonny, of World Cup fame, was not actually in his 2004 England team.

Woodward apparently asked the television crew if they could run that question through again. He threatened to ruin the whole interview with a string of obscenities. Sir Clive said: "We'll have to, or I'll swear. I'll say f***** f***** f***** f*****" The crew sportingly agreed to repeat the previous question and answer. I'd have preferred the original version.

2004

A bold admission

It was a bold thing for TV3's news presenter Mike McRoberts to own up to the other day. In a weekend paper, Mike was asked for "three secrets" the public didn't know about him.

So Mike offered the story of him once being a senior club player in Christchurch. He said that he was once captain of a team that was beaten 121-0. He reckoned it's still some sort of horror record for the club. "At one stage I saw someone warming up and hoped it was going to be much-needed relief," he said. "But it was a touch judge, replacing one who'd pulled a hamstring running to the tryline all the time."

2004

Where were you?

Where were you when you heard about the horrors of September 11? Or when Elvis died? Or John Lennon? Well, for the sake of getting All Black history right (and to justify an hour of doodling on the Internet), here is the list of responses from a recent batch of new All Blacks when asked that beautiful question: "Where were you when you heard you'd been selected for the All Blacks?"

Conrad Smith – at home, via a text message from his mate. Smith immediately had to cancel an overseas holiday and get a haircut.

_____

Jimmy Cowan – about to tee it up with his dad at a golf course.

_____

Steven Bates – also playing golf, at a sponsor's day.

_____

Piri Weepu – at Rugby League Park in Wellington (bizarrely, it is the training headquarters of the Wellington NPC squad).

_____

Saimone Taumoepeau – at his workplace, in a cardboard box-making factory in Auckland.

_____

Casey Laulala – sipping soft drinks in a hotel at Sheffield, central Canterbury.

_____

Luke McAlister – at home with his parents and his partner, Brooke.

_____

Jerome Kaino – also at home, and according to reports – probably exaggerated – he was sewing up a pair of pants when he heard the news.

2006

The most awful match

A couple of years ago Peter FitzSimons, writing in the *Sydney Morning Herald*, took up the challenge of recalling the worst game he ever played in.

He came up with one between New South Wales and our very own and much-loved Counties in the mid-1980s. (For those who may have forgotten, FitzSimons was an international lock for several years and gained notoriety for several reasons: for his ability in the knuckle area; and because he once played a game for Australia, to which his paper sent no journalist — the game was in Canada — so he filed a match report to his editor.)

Back to the Counties game: "The mud was six inches thick and it stank," wrote Fitz. "These enormous Kiwis — shearers all, with legs like oak trees and arms like pistons — kept coming and coming and coming, wave after wave after wave, until we felt like a tiny island in a hurricane, lost somewhere in the South Pacific and wishing mum was there.

"I hated every minute of it, played like a dog but was named man of the match, which came with an enormous sheepskin rug. Despite that, Tizza, our coach, was on to me and I was, quite rightly, dropped from the side. Within 20 minutes of the match finishing, my sheepskin draped around my shoulders, still arguing furiously, I sank beneath the waves."

Hey, hey, hey

It was Justin Marshall who passed the ball to Zinzan Brooke for Zinny to launch his famous drop goal in the test against South Africa at Pretoria in 1996. I asked Marshall: "In all that noise, what did Zinny shout to you to let you know he wanted the ball?"

Marshall replied: "Well, he didn't yell out 'give it to me' or anything like that. All he said was 'hey, hey, hey!' So I passed it to him and the rest is history."

Taylor comes clean

Not so long ago on *The Rugby Channel* was a Celtic League match from Newport, Wales, between the Llanelli Scarlets and the Newport Dragons.

You'll have to pardon me for coming over all misty-eyed when I noted that the game was played at the Rodney Parade Ground. This venerable rugby arena has changed little in the past 100 years. The All Blacks first played there in 1905-06.

To my eye the jammed-together houses along the streets behind the main grandstand have hardly altered either. Seeing them again on television reminded me of the time in 1978, when facilities at the ground were not what they ought to have been.

In the New Zealand dressing room there were no hot showers, and the game had just finished on a particularly muddy field. Yet this did not bother All Black Mark Taylor. Still in his playing strip, Taylor walked out into the street, selected a house and knocked on the door. The local housewife took pity on him when he asked if she would mind if he came in and had a bath.

"No problems," she said. Taylor emerged 20 minutes later clean and scrubbed, and no doubt grateful for the famous Newport rugby hospitality.

1978

Great Grand Slammers

We recall proudly that the 1995 All Blacks scored an "away" Grand Slam of wins at the World Cup in South Africa. Sean Fitzpatrick's team beat Ireland 43-19, Wales 34-9, Scotland 48-30 and England 45-29. That makes it a unique Grand Slam by any country over the British and Irish teams. Australia achieved their only one in 1984 and South Africa's most recent was in 1961. Graham Mourie's 1978 All Blacks were New Zealand Grand Slammers, as were Tana Umaga's 2005 team.

But let's add to those facts. The Springboks can still claim the best Grand Slam results. Their 1912-13 and 1951-52 teams beat the four nations that are traditionally called Grand Slam opponents, and also beat France, so compiling quintuple Grand Slams.

2005

Martin's musings

When Martin Johnson toured New Zealand last year we found him an informed after-dinner speaker. We got a few laughs from him, but mostly it was the straight-talking Martin we met.

He is perhaps more of a dag when another writer puts a spin on his words. These quotes come from a recent interview Johnson gave to the eminent Donald McRae in *The Guardian*:

Johnson told McRae: "I went out to New Zealand in 1989 and got picked for the New Zealand Under-21s. I was in Wellington at the time because I needed a visa for the trip to Australia, and I sat in this motel watching the news. I couldn't believe it. They interrupted the national news and some guy says, 'We've just been handed the New Zealand Under-21 side'.

"Can you imagine them announcing the England Under-21 side on TV – never mind in the middle of the news?

"Who knows what would have happened if I'd stayed [in New Zealand]? But I was only 20 and would have had to move to a bigger province [from King Country] to challenge locks like Ian Jones and Robin Brooke. They weren't bad players, those two, so I would've had my work cut out."

2005

London 2005. An interview with Martin Johnson. You can see why so many people looked up to that man.

They said it

"Would it help if I put 'sold' signs around their necks?" – *rugby league coach Graham Lowe, at the 1990 All Black trials after Alex Wyllie jokingly asked him which players he wanted.*

"I'll be disappointed if we don't have eight wins." – *Welsh rugby team assistant coach Derek Quinnell, on the eve of Wales' ill-fated eight-match 1988 New Zealand tour. Wales eventually won two matches.*

"I'm still an amateur, of course, but I became rugby's first millionaire five years ago." – *David Campese in 1991.*

"You'd better count the players. I think Meads might have eaten one." – *Kel Tremain recalls the comment of a linesman to the referee during the torrid Hawke's Bay-King Country Ranfurly Shield match in 1969, which the Bay won 19-16.*

"Be careful with that water, or you'll turn him into paste." – *Referee Clive Norling, to a St John ambulanceman during the South Africa-New Zealand test at Eden Park in 1981, after prop Gary Knight had been knocked out by a flour bomb dropped from a low-flying plane.*

"You're not getting too old to play rugby are you? It is terrible, isn't it, when you get past it." – *Prince Charles, to All Black captain Sean Fitzpatrick while touring New Zealand in 1994.*

"Playing the All Blacks is like being in an out-of-control washing machine, afloat with 100 football boots." – *Wallaby lock Peter FitzSimons in 2000.*

"I don't know about us not having a Plan B when things went wrong, we looked like we didn't have a Plan A." – *England coach Geoff Cooke, after England had been humbled by New Zealand in the 1995 World Cup semi-final.*

Anton speaks for us all

Forget about the squabble between Anton Oliver and Laurie Mains, as detailed in Anton's book in 2005. Or the fact that All Blacks have been known to down a few milkshakes at their after-match parties. The biggest relief to all rugby males from Anton's ramblings came not from his book but from a profile about him written by his friend, artist Grahame Sydney. In the *Sunday Star-Times* story Anton came out of the closet about a much more important issue.

Said the craggy Anton: 'No-one has ever managed to convince me that making your bed every day is important. So I don't. It stays unmade, because I haven't found a good argument as to why it matters."

Thank God someone has had the guts to front the world on this all-important subject. For years we Kiwi blokes have wanted a spokesman to lead the way for us on this question. Now we have one.

I say: "Bloody brilliant mate!" How many decent New Zealand blokes have fought for years with their partners, their mothers, and even themselves over this issue of straightening the sheets and covers (and even getting "hospital corners" just right)? Now we have Anton as our stated leader.

When nature calls

Many of us saw Jerry Collins wee-wee on the field before kick-off in the Tri-Nations match against Australia in Christchurch. But Jerry's act was hardly the most shocking ever seen in New Zealand history. The 1961 French team had a player take a necessary leak against a goal-post at training in Nelson. I recall this only because it invoked a classic piece of rugby writing by the immortal T P McLean. In his book of the tour, T P wrote: "At the team's first practice in New Zealand, on the grounds of Nelson College, where thousands of boys have been enjoined to behave like gentlemen at all stages of their lives, the French hooker Jacques Rollett, at the call of nature proceeded to unbehave like a gentleman. A goal-post was handy, so at the urging of some atavistically canine impulse, he nobly did his duty by it."

2006

Fiji hit rock bottom

How pathetically sad for rugby that Fiji dissolved so meekly against the All Blacks at Albany Stadium last weekend. The 91-0 game was a serious mismatch from just after kick-off and it became a squirming embarrassment to watch. I very much admire John Drake as a TV match pundit but I could not go along with his summation of Fiji as being "a better team than this" as the score mounted. I've never seen a worse Fiji team.

Having said that, congratulations must go to Greg Somerville, the Canterbury and Crusaders prop, who scored his first test try in his – wait for it – 42nd test. The burly former Wairoa man travels through life, I understand, being called "Yoda" by those who know him best. That name comes from a wise, short, squat *Star Wars* film character whom Somerville is said to resemble.

In *Star Wars* Yoda also waited a long time to make his mark in life. But he always spoke with great commonsense and coined several famous catch-phrases that might apply to Greg Somerville. "May the force be with you," is the most famous. In *Return of the Jedi* Yoda also said, "Do, or do not – there is no try", which I guess could apply to Somerville's previous lack of tries.

2005 🏉

Of roasts and boil-ups

There's a vast amount of advice available on diet these days. Rugby players seem to be forever being advised about what is good for them and what's not. Many teams have dietary advisors.

But while you can tell the lads over and over what is preferable to munch on, they still have minds of their own. Take the profiles of the New Zealand Maori players, shown on Maori TV before the team's 2004 games in North America. Listed as "most favourite food" were such delights as mum's roasts, nana's roasts, KFC, pizza, pies, McDonald's and fish 'n chips.

Of those I noted, only flanker Wayne Ormond listed "hangi" as his favourite food. Prop Deacon Manu listed "boil-up" as his personal pick. The team coaches, Matt Te Pou and Hika Reid, put "kaimoana" (seafood) and "terotero" (pig intestines) at the top of their lists.

A great servant of the game

Some words here about the 1950s All Black captain Bob Stuart, who passed away last week in Wellington.

The *New Zealand Herald* rightly called him a "proud wearer of the silver fern", but the quiet, dignified and ever-courteous Stuart gave service to the game in areas that were much more significant than his time as a player, even if he did captain the 1953-54 All Blacks to the United Kingdom.

Stuart was a 35-year-old "coaching advisor" of the All Blacks in 1956 during the epic series against the Springboks. He was called in to help toughen up the New Zealand forward effort midway through the four-test series. This was achieved by bringing in hard-man prop Kevin Skinner for the third test and thus a powerful All Black legend was born.

After that Bob Stuart's commitment to rugby further intensified. He was Canterbury's coach when they beat the Lions in 1959 and was the shrewd instigator of something that has become synonymous with our national style since – the second five-eighth cutting back inside to be tackled and create a new ruck.

As an administrator Stuart rose to be the New Zealand Rugby Union's deputy chairman and had 15 years on the board, earning life membership. He was also the New Zealand delegate to the International Rugby Board for many years. Even after his time as a delegate was over he continued to work for that body, most notably in the expanding of the IRB executive, increasing the membership of countries, simplifying the laws of the game and re-writing much of the heavy wording of the law book.

The headline about him being a proud wearer of All Black colours is far too simple. Rugby meant much more than that to Bob Stuart.

2005

A day at Jade Stadium

Notes from a visit to Christchurch in 2005.

To go to a game in Christchurch these days is to experience many contrasts. The luxury of the new grandstand at Jade Stadium gives a perfect view, though it is higher and further from the field than at Wellington's Westpac Stadium.

It was a first for me to be asked to pass the bottles of white and red wine back and forth along the row of seats from friends who have been sitting in the same seats for years.

Some of the people around me did not watch the game much at all. Instead they caught up with the week's chatter and natter ("Did you know that so-and-so is remarrying his wife? Weren't they divorced years ago?"). And when full attention was given to the rugby, the crowd chanted for "Caaaanter-bree!" instead of "Crusaders", who were playing.

Don't get me wrong: I enjoyed the company. The difference came when I battled past a sturdy doorman to enter the post-match Canterbury Supporters' Club function. There, the great Dick Tayler – he of 1974 Christchurch Commonwealth Games fame – is president.

The room was so crowded that Dick has a roped off area he calls his "corporate box", and entry is only by Dick's all-powerful invitation.

To shoosh the crowd for the after-match speeches, he bellowed "sha-daaap!" into the microphone, adding: "If you want to talk you can clear off outside!"

I was invited on to the podium to represent those who had any association with the beaten Hurricanes. The people were great – they listened attentively and roared at every reference I made about the strengths of the Hurricanes' franchise. They cheered when I told them I had witnessed many great Canterbury moments over the years, including Wayne Smith's try when Canterbury lifted the Ranfurly Shield off Wellington in 1982. I added: "To us in Wellington that clearly came from a forward pass." That comment drew raucous booing. It was good, earthy fun.

I left the clubrooms soon after to another strange sound. It was the Crusaders supporters, clutching their beers and cheering the Blues' efforts in Sydney as they tried to beat back the Waratahs. Has such a sound ever been heard from Canterbury rugby people before?

A memory to treasure

Keith Quinn

Ayliffe Taylor — memories to last a life-time.

One afternoon, not even a month ago, Wellington journalist Joseph Romanos and I travelled an hour north to visit 84-year-old Mrs Ayliffe Taylor, of Waikanae. She welcomed us warmly into her home and offered us tea and tiny cakes in the grand old style.

"Call me Ayliffe," she insisted, and we settled in to hear her family's story. You see, Ayliffe was the daughter of Arthur Harding, who was a member of the Great Britain rugby team to New Zealand in 1904. He was also in the 1905 Welsh team that scored the famous 3-0 win over the All Blacks in Cardiff, and was the captain of the 1908 Anglo-Welsh team to New Zealand.

On his first visit to our country, Arthur met Miss Winifred Wilford, of Wellington, and a friendship started. The two exchanged letters. Ayliffe thought that on his return in 1908 the two became "betrothed" in some way. The Welshman immigrated to New Zealand in 1910 and married Miss Wilford in 1915.

Ayliffe was born in 1920. To hear her connection with the past was a privilege. It was a lovely afternoon, spent in a gracious lady's company.

As Romanos and I drove home we marvelled at her sprightly nature and excellent memory of her father. I am very glad I snapped off a couple of photographs of Ayliffe as she chatted away and looked at her father's scrapbook of the tour. That's because last week, quite suddenly, her health took a turn for the worse and she passed away.

Now though, at least we have her family's recall of the man himself. He didn't have much to do with the game once he landed in New Zealand, though he coached for a time at Martinborough. Ayliffe said: "We had a farm near the Lochore family in Wairarapa. Brian will remember him."

2005

Lock the gates

A great media quote from 2005. While broadcasting the stop-start go-nowhere Highlanders-Bulls game from Carisbrook, commentator Paul Allison summed things up succinctly: "[This game] is so terrible they've locked the gates to keep the crowd inside."

It was also great to hear in the same broadcast former All Black Tony Kreft adding his wisdom. I haven't set eyes on Tony since Grahame Thorne arranged a dinner with him in Auckland a few years back. "It's a BYO restaurant," said Thorney, whereupon as an Aucklander he delicately selected a couple of bottles of fine wine, chosen to match the subtleties of the restaurant's menu. Tony Kreft, on the other hand, fresh in town from Ranfurly in Central Otago, shocked the staff by putting under our table a dozen large bottles of beer.

Common courtesy prevents me from relating how many bottles Tony drank that night, except to say I was amazed.

The case of the exploding boots

Wilson Whineray tells a story about one of the most amusing sights he saw on a rugby field. It happened during the All Black tour of South Africa in 1960.

"Don Clarke was a giant figure in our team," says Whineray. "His massive kicking intimidated opposition and was a real match-winner. There was always a lot of fuss about Don's boots. They were precious to us.

"We got to the ground before one test and Don opened his gear bag in the dressing room and said with horror, 'I've left my boots back at the hotel'. This was a tragedy. Someone was dispatched to race back to fetch them, but in the meantime the game had to begin.

"What was Don to do? It so happened that Kel Tremain always carried a second pair of boots. It was a suspicion of his. He didn't intend using them, so it didn't matter what sort of condition they were in, as long as he had a second pair in his bag.

"He pulled out his second pair. They were dirty, old, worn, with the stitching ripped. He said, 'Here, "Camel", you can use these if you like'.

"So Don pulled on Kel's second pair and out on to the field we trotted. We hadn't been going more than a few minutes when we were given a penalty, just inside Don's range. He placed the ball, took his full run-up and really launched into his kick. As he kicked the ball, there was a sort of explosion. The ball went one way and pieces of the boot flew in all directions. Kel's ancient boot hadn't been able to withstand Don's kicking power and had disintegrated. We nearly fell over laughing."

J G D, of Dunedin, remembers another boots story, told to him by a visiting priest. Friends of the priest bought two tickets from the All Black team before the first test against the British Lions in 1971. When picking up the tickets on the morning of the game – from Larry Salmon, the team's masseur – the priest was told of the plight of that year's New Zealand No 8, Alan Sutherland.

Apparently, Sutherland had left a pair of boots to dry overnight on a heater in his hotel room. They were ruined, of course.

On the morning of the game Sutherland had to scour the shops of Dunedin for a new pair. Happily he found some. But midway through the second half a desperate clearing kick slid off the side of Sutherland's boot and Scottish prop "Mighty Mouse" McLauchlan charged down the kick and scored the game's only try.

The Lions won 9-3 and went on to win the series.

The morals of these stories might be: always remember rugby stories and pass them on to the next generation. And: be careful with your boots – they could decide the outcome of a test series.

Joseph Romanos Collection

"The Boot" Don Clarke lines up another shot at goal.

Dancing All Blacks

Everyone is excited by former All Black hooker Norm Hewitt's success in *Dancing with the Stars*. Norm was brilliant on the dance floor and looked as pretty as a picture in doing his thing. But last week I took time to read the New Zealand Sports Hall of Fame's latest publication, called *Billy's Trip Home*, and found out that All Blacks have been dancing in the spotlight for years.

The book is a faithful reproduction of the letters sent home as stories for the *Southland Times* by the Southland All Black Billy Stead, as he travelled the world with the 1905-06 All Blacks. The reports have been shaped into book form and are a delight to read. The dancing bit that caught my eye came as the team, under skipper Dave Gallaher, made the six-week sea journey to Britain.

In the evenings dances were put on aboard ship. Unfortunately for the 26 members of the touring party, there were only six "eligible" young ladies to dance with. Stead's story does not mention if the women were exhausted as they whirled around the dance floor. But he does say that "dummies" were supplied by the crew to make up the dancing partners for team members.

I'll bet the hookers of that famous team danced with the dummies, as did, of course, fast-breaking halfbacks. They've been involved in selling dummies for years.

2005

Spot a chink, do a jink

Here are a couple of leftovers from the 2005 World Cup sevens in Hong Kong. I know I waxed rhapsodic about the superb event and Fiji's wonderful win. In case you doubted my impartiality, this is what the eminent Peter FitzSimons told his *Sydney Morning Herald* readers:

"Among other things, I felt privileged to be able to watch the Fiji sevens team in action. Forget science, forget precisely worked-out patterns of attack and minutely-calibrated defence, forget dull percentage play worked out by slide rule and logarithmic tables. This was no less than high art, as the men in the white jerseys moved the ball around, probing for the gap – probing, probing, probing – until suddenly one of them would spot a chink, do a jink, then do a high-risk behind-the-back flick pass to nail the blind winger 20 metres to his left.

"When these moves worked, there was a wonderful try. When they didn't, no worries, they cleaned up the disaster, and kept going. For pure spectating pleasure, watching the Fijians play sevens is about as good as it gets, on the grounds that they play the game the way it was meant to be played."

Still reading, Matt?

Writing in Britain's *Sunday Times* in January 2005, Paul Forsyth might have slightly caught out that year's Scottish rugby coach, the Australian-born Matt Williams.

Forsyth wrote: "In an Irish interview 18 months ago, when asked about his reading habits, Matt Williams said he was in the middle of a book about Alexander the Great. Last Friday, he confirmed his voracious appetite for the printed word, explaining that his passion was for sport, business and 'trashy' novelists. 'And, at the moment, I'm reading some really good stuff on Alexander the Great.'"

Did that mean Williams took 18 months to finish the book he had on Alexander the Great?

Mind you, credit to Williams for this quote from the same story: "The best team never wins the World Cup. That's apart from the All Blacks in 1987. England weren't the best team in the 2003 World Cup."

An age-old rivalry

Don't you just love the centuries-old rugby rivalry between England and Scotland? Over recent years the Scots have had to bite the bullet many times when playing their old rivals. It would not have helped ease centuries of bitterness when the Scots noted an outrageous imbalance in national representation in the team chosen by Englishman Clive Woodward for the 2005 Lions team – three Scots and 21 Englishmen in the original tour party.

That's why there's always particular relish in Scottish rugby circles when the tables are turned in the Six Nations Championship, and against the odds Scotland win the Calcutta Cup. The poets, bards and wordsmiths from North o' the Border come out from "yonder hills" and offer ringing peels of praise to the Scottish boys.

This poem is as I received it from Robyn Murray, of Tillicoultry, 45 minutes north of Edinburgh, with minor amendments for decency's sake.

Ode to English rugby 2006

Ye came up here tae paradise, tae beat us at your game,
Aw wind and piss and full o' shite, you're aw the bloody same,
Ye ca yerselves the champions, the nation's most elite,
*But now Scotland are the champions, you've just been f****** beat.*

A game that wis invented, fur English gentlemen,
Not for Highland Jocks wi tartan frocks; but think a-bloody-gain,
A ball that's shape't like an egg, is just a stupit farse,
But a' suppose it makes it easier, tae ram right up your arse.

So git back hame an lick yer wounds, yee bunch o' stupit fools,
*It's time fur you tae cheat again, and change the f****** rules,*
Rugby, fitba, cricket too, you're just a shower o chancers,
*Stick tae whit ye do the best, you morris f****** dancers!*

The worst weather days

I see the Planet-Rugby365 website has a historical piece about occasions when weather conditions have disrupted significant rugby games. The story follows the 2006 "foggy final" of the Super 14 in Christchurch. I note that they've neglected to mention two infamous bad-weather days in New Zealand rugby history.

One of them was the windy day at Athletic Park in 1961, when the All Blacks beat France 5-3. Winds roared in at more than 140 miles an hour that day. And no mention was made of the 2005 test at Jade Stadium in Christchurch, when rain bucketed down in freezing torrents.

There was also only modest reference made to the notorious 1975 "water polo" test in Auckland, when New Zealand played Scotland.

There was no reference either to the gloomy All Blacks-Scotland game at Edinburgh in 1978, when arctic darkness spread over the city from early-afternoon. That was the day All Black centre Bruce Robertson scored a vital try late in the second half and as he ran back watched his captain, Graham Mourie, approach Bryan Williams and say: "Great try, Beegee."

Here is a list of the worst playing conditions for big games in New Zealand rugby history (it does beg the question of whether Christchurch, with its appalling record, deserves to be allocated major matches!):

1. **THE COLDEST** – All Blacks v Lions, Christchurch, 2005.
2. **THE FOGGIEST** – Crusaders v Hurricanes, Christchurch, 2006.
3. **THE WETTEST I** – All Blacks v Wallabies (Tri Nations), Christchurch, 2002.
4. **THE WETTEST II** – New Zealand v Scotland, Auckland, 1975.
5. **THE WINDIEST** – All Blacks v France, Wellington, 1961.
6. **THE MUDDIEST I** – Junior All Blacks v Lions, Wellington, 1966.
7. **THE MUDDIEST II** – All Blacks v Lions, Christchurch, 1977.
8. **THE SNOWIEST** – Southland v Manawatu (Ranfurly Shield), Invercargill, 1939.
9. **THE SUNNIEST** – No winner in this category, because all games seem to be played at night these days.
10. **THE SLIPPERIEST** – Canterbury v Wellington (Ranfurly Shield), Christchurch, 2001 (the conditions were actually fine – it's just that Steve Walsh's refereeing looked slippery to we Wellingtonians!).

2006

Broadcasting heroes

My two rugby broadcasting heroes were Winston McCarthy and Bill McLaren.

Top: The young Quinn listens and learns at a farewell function in Wellington for the incomparable McCarthy, who was the voice of All Black rugby for so long, and who helped me in my early broadcasting years.

Bottom: Photographed with the peerless Scottish rugby commentator Bill McLaren at the Hong Kong sevens in 1990.

Oysters, beer and the Bledisloe Cup

In 1951 the folks at that fine old rugby club at Bluff were delighted when one of their number, flanker Eddie Robinson, made the All Black team for a vital Bledisloe Cup game at the Sydney Cricket Ground. Eddie was their first All Black.

So pleased were club members that two sizeable buckets of fresh Bluff oysters were dispatched to Sydney. Travel in those days was not like it is today, so the oysters, carefully addressed to Mr Eddie Robinson, New Zealand Rugby Team, c/- Sydney Cricket Ground, went by train and plane to Wellington and thence by flying boat to Sydney. There, an honest Sydney taxi driver drove through pouring rain to the SCG, where the two packets were placed outside the All Blacks' dressing room door. The test had started.

The team came off the field covered in mud, 8-0 victors over Australia. Thus New Zealand regained the Bledisloe Cup. The All Black hooker that day was Norm Wilson, who once told me: "We brought the cup into the dressing room, then we poured Eddie's two buckets of oysters into it. Beer was added in abundance and the most glorious, celebratory Bledisloe Cup cocktail was passed around."

2004

And what of India?

When the 2006 *New Zealand Rugby Almanack* hit the stands it was, as usual, crammed with every scrap of rugby information you could possibly want, if only to settle those friendly arguments.

The editors threw in this withering gem. You recall those tiresome British writers reporting the "raping and pillaging" that New Zealand rugby presumes it can do to the three major Pacific nations? Well, store this one away: of the 1064 All Blacks there have been in our history, 14 have been born in Samoa, eight in Fiji and seven in Tonga. By contrast, 15 players from England have been born in India. The almanack sums up: "One could cynically ask what England has done for Indian rugby?"

Jeff Young and his jaw

Sad to note the recent passing of the Welsh and Lions forward Jeff Young. He was a 23-test veteran as a hooker, when 23 caps was a seriously high total. He toured with the Lions to South Africa in 1968 and came to New Zealand with Wales in 1969. The RAF man was an excellent player and by all accounts a very decent man.

But in the 500-page *The Complete Who's Who of International Rugby*, the only line of description about Jeff Young's playing career states: "RAF. Jaw broken by Colin Meads NZ v Wales 1969."

I remember the incident clearly. It was at the test in Christchurch. Welsh players learnt that day that no player should jersey-pull an All Black while in close proximity to Colin Meads. Mind you, not everyone saw Meads as the bad guy. Welsh supporters and their media wailed at Meads for supposedly swinging a fist into Young's face, but the honest New Zealand fans saw it differently.

A really, really clever line did the rounds was that Jeff Young "shouldn't have deliberately rammed his jaw into Pinetree's fist!"

2005

Baboons 2, Force 0

This from the Western Force's Internet site.

In 2006 it appeared that two players in the Force squad, Dave Pocock and Brock James, were relaxing in their hotel rooms when the team had a couple of days' R and R at the Sun City resort. The two players were startled when two baboons invited themselves into the room through open windows. One of the animals helped itself to a sandwich off a plate. There was a moment of real anxiety when the animal got entangled in the room's curtains. One of the players was snoozing and was startled, to say the least, when he awoke to see a baboon staring at him from the nearby window sill.

The only New Zealand story I can recall that is vaguely comparable concerns the prominent Kiwi media man who asked to be changed to another hotel room, complaining that he did not like the way the pigeons on the ledge outside his room were always looking at him.

Two to remember

I don't spend all my time in cemeteries, but I made a point of visiting these two graves.

Left: In Menton, France, at the gravesite of William Webb Ellis, who may or may not have picked up the ball and run with it in 1823.

Below: Doing a story from Dave Gallaher's gravesite at the Nine Elms cemetery in Poperinge, Belgium. He was the 1905-06 Originals All Black captain and gave his life in World War I.

The day the students humiliated the Springboks

The death of Brian "B B J" Fitzpatrick in October 2006 brought back memories of the time when, as a lad, I was privileged to see him play in one of the country's greatest games – the 1956 clash between New Zealand University and the Springboks on a warm, sunny afternoon at Athletic Park.

Fitzpatrick was in the University team that scored a famous 22-15 win. I recall several significant things from the game. The first was that I went to see the action with my mother. She was a stickler for school attendance, but as the game was played on a Wednesday she must have understood that her nine-year-old son had an obsession with the game even then. Somehow she wheedled me the day off from my primary school lessons.

Then there was the corner-to-corner runaway try by Auckland midfielder John Tanner. Thinking back, he ran 70 metres (yards then) from at least his own "25". Tanner and Fitzpatrick had been in the 1953-54 All Blacks team to Europe, but were ignored by the national selectors afterwards.

Then there was the famous try-that-wasn't by Wellington star Ron Jarden. The left winger zig-zagged his way through the Springbok defence from the halfway line and was mobbed by the crowd when he touched down behind the northern goalposts. Alas, the touch judge, the renowned Eric Tindill, had his flag up back at halfway. Jarden had touched the sideline with a boot. But it didn't stop us roaring our approval. In that year anything that humiliated the Springboks, even tries that were disallowed, was cheered.

University rugby was very strong then. Brian Fitzpatrick had been part of a Victoria University club lineup that included four All Blacks – Fitzpatrick, Jarden, Jim Fitzgerald and Bill Clark. One time, in 1954 I think it was, 24,000 turned up to watch their Jubilee Cup final against the equally-powerful Petone club, led by All Blacks Bob Scott, Don McIntosh and mercurial should-have-been-an-All Black Jackie Dougan. It's sad to think we don't see club games like that any more.

Sevens Heaven

It's intriguing to note the gold medal-winning sevens teams for New Zealand in the last three Commonwealth Games, and the number of All Blacks involved.

KUALA LUMPUR, 1998: **Eric Rush (captain), Dallas Seymour, Jonah Lomu, Caleb Ralph, Amasio Valence, Rico Gear, Christian Cullen, Joeli Vidiri, Bruce Reihana, Roger Randle.**

MANCHESTER, 2002: **Eric Rush (captain), Chris Masoe, Amasio Valence, Roger Randle, Mils Muliaina, Craig de Goldi, Anthony Tuitavake, Brad Fleming, Rodney So'oialo, Bruce Reihana, Craig Newby, Karl Tenana.**

MELBOURNE, 2006: **Tafai Ioasa (captain), Cory Jane, Amasio Valence, Josh Blackie, Lote Raikabula, Liam Messam, Tamati Ellison, Alando Soakai, Soseni Anese, Nigel Hunt, Tanerau Latimer, Onosai Tololima-Auva'a.**

Of the winning 2006 squad only Sosene Anese has played for the All Blacks so far. It will be interesting to see if any of his team-mates can make the step up.

Blame it on the French

There has been a huge rise in demand for "morning after" contraceptive pills the day after rugby internationals in Britain. This fact has been particularly noted in Dublin, of all places. The thrill of the rugby occasion obviously affects the amorous inclinations of rugby fans and followers.

In Dublin a check has even been made to see if there is more demand when certain countries' followers come to down.

So which country invokes the most requests for the pill at local clinics after Irish home tests? Why, France, of course.

An unworthy nil

Just as Lindsay Knight writes caringly about the Ranfurly Shield, Don Cameron loves the Barbarians, and men like Geoff Miller, Clive Akers, Paul Neazor and Peter Marriott are amazed by rugby statistics, old Keith Quinn here claims with chest-thumping pride to be the only writer worldwide who has regularly written about the honourable rugby score of nil. I ask: does the South African effort of achieving nil against Australia in 2006 (49-0) fall into the "worthy" category of nil scores?

As the self-declared world authority, I say "No". A commendable nil is one achieved only after a gutsy 80-minute effort, when players have given their best, where there has been commitment, courage, bravery and rugby valour. Sadly I saw none of that from South Africa in Brisbane. They were instead something akin to a rugby rabble and sometimes they strayed outside the game's code of decency – evidenced by Victor Matfield's yellow card and Enrico Januarie's "facial" on Stirling Mortlock.

For the best nil score in New Zealand rugby I go back to the 12-0 defeat of New Zealand by Munster in 1978. At least New Zealand never gave up that day. They were stunned and hugely disappointed, but they held their heads up throughout and battled hard against the mighty Munstermen. The singing afterwards by the New Zealanders at the joyous Munster celebrations was a brilliant observance that they accepted the score, tough though it might have been to chew on.

New Zealand have not achieved a nil score in a test match for more than 40 years. But their 0-0 draw with Scotland early in 1964, while not remembered as a great game, was a gritty contest, thrilling all the way. Scotland battled away, trying to score their first win over New Zealand. The New Zealand effort was gripping, too, as they tried to hold on grimly to their unbeaten test record on that tour.

But a major test team like South Africa suffering a 49-0 loss to a team that many predicted they would beat? No way does South Africa make my list of great rugby efforts for nil return.

NOTE: the Springboks' previous nil score in a test was 28-0, against New Zealand at Carisbrook in 1999.

2006

They said it

"I remember calling him 'Sir' once." – *Keith Lawrence, recalling his rep debut as a referee in a King Country-Thames Valley match. He was 26 and in awe of 35-year-old Colin Meads.*

"If you can't take a punch, you should play table tennis." – *French coach Pierre Berbizier, following Scotland's accusations of French foul play in 1995.*

"This looks a good team on paper, let's see how it looks on grass." – *Nigel Melville, in 1984 on England's new-look team to play Australia.*

"The relationship between the Welsh and the English is based on trust and understanding. They don't trust us and we don't understand them." – *English rugby official Dudley Wood in 1986.*

"Remember that rugby is a team game; all 14 of you make sure you pass the ball to Jonah." – *Supporter's fax to All Blacks before 1995 World Cup semi-final against England.*

"Colin Meads is the kind of player you expect to see emerging from a ruck with the remains of a jockstrap between his teeth." – *Tony O'Reilly, who played for Ireland and the Lions from 1955-70.*

"Most unfortunate match ever played... Bad enough having to play a team officially designated **NZ Natives**, but spectacle thousands Europeans frantically cheering on band of coloured men to defeat members of own race too much for the **Springboks** who frankly disgusted." – *South African press correspondent Charles Blackett's cabled report of the NZ Maori-Springbok match at Napier in 1921.*

"Grandmother or tails, sir?" – *Referee to Princess Anne's son Peter Phillips, Gordonstoun School's rugby captain, before a coin toss in 1995.*

Choosing the right entrance

Peter Bush captured this classic photo of Pope John Paul II at Lancaster Park in 1986. Nothing but the players' entry for the Pope!

Zut alors! Time for revenge

The sensational consequences after Italian soccer player Marco Materazzi allegedly insulted Zinedine Zidane's mother and sister during the 2006 soccer World Cup final reminded me of an incident from my time as a touring rugby commentator. For obvious reasons, there'll be "no names, no pack drill" in the following story.

In the 1980s, on an All Black tour of France, a young Frenchwoman was very distressed at the after-match function of a regional game. A concerned All Black player asked why. "My husband, 'ee plays against you today but I know 'ee is 'aving an affair. I am going to show 'eem what it's like to 'ave zee boot on zee other foot. I am going to 'ave an affair myself tonight." The All Black gallantly offered to assist her in that matter and the pair left the function, with obvious intent.

Six years later, on the next All Black tour of France, at another regional XV game an almighty fight broke out shortly after kick-off. In the commentary area none of us could understand what had caused the sudden explosion of violence. It wasn't until later that the word was whispered that in the French XV that day was the "wronged" husband of the previous tour. Apparently he had seen who had left the after match-function with his wife and now, six years later, seeing the same man marking him in this game, decided to exact his revenge.

Getting the best out of Tana

Well done Phil Gifford for his quirky *Front Row Rugby Show* spot on Radio Sport. Each week Phil rings various rugby personalities and asks them 10 questions. Included in the interview is an offer to play the interview subject's all-time favourite song. One time on the "Ten and a Song" segment Phil secured a real scoop – an interview with the normally very private Tana Umaga. And what things we learned about the former All Black captain!

Like how Tana uses facial moisturiser from time to time, how his favourite holiday spot in New Zealand is Kerikeri, and the grumpiest player he ever marked was the Springbok, Marius Joubert. His favourite players while growing up were his brother Mike (the Samoan international) and Stu Wilson and Bernie Fraser. When asked about the worst item of clothing he had owned, Tana recalled once wearing a corduroy shirt, bought in Italy, that had tassels and metal studs and was done all in a country and western style. "I don't know what I was thinking when I bought it," he said.

His favourite song turned out to be an intriguing choice. "I know all the words to it," he said, "and several times on tour the boys asked me to sing it, so I did." The song? The 1985 Live Aid theme song "Do they know it's Christmas?"

2006

The wrong Robinson

The celebrity oops of the media in 2006 would have to go to the New Zealand edition of *New Idea* magazine. Apparently 1997-2001 All Black Mark "Sharkey" Robinson, who plays his rugby in Northampton, England, was seen in the company of one of the world's rising young actresses. She has been described as "a British-born Hollywood starlet", and goes by the name of Mischa Barton.

At one stage the oft-photographed young lady was in the company of our Sharkey. Their meeting and friendly poses rated big news in Britain. Cameras clicked and the gossip columnists attempted to find out more about this stylish couple.

Maybe *New Idea* was not on the receiving list of any of the couple's pictures. Notwithstanding, the magazine instead decided to graphically position the handsome couple together.

However, the Mark Robinson who was depicted, posing helpfully in his All Black uniform, was not Mark Darren Robinson, known to all as Sharkey. Instead it was Mark Powell Robinson, the 2000-02 All Black, who is happily married and works as the New Zealand Rugby Union talent identification manager.

The first XV of fields

In June 2006 the Taranaki Rugby Union hosted the Japan-Samoa test at its headquarters at Yarrow Stadium. That completed the first XV of New Zealand rugby's official test grounds. In alphabetical order the other grounds have been:

Albany	North Harbour Stadium (6 New Zealand tests)
Auckland	Eden Park (58 New Zealand tests and 4 others)
	Epsom Showgrounds (1 New Zealand test)
	Potter's Park (1 New Zealand test)
Christchurch	Lancaster Park/Jade Stadium (43 New Zealand tests and 2 others)
Dunedin	Tahuna Park (1 New Zealand test)
	Carisbrook
	(34 New Zealand tests and 3 others)
Hamilton	Rugby Park/Waikato Stadium (5 New Zealand tests and 1 other)
Invercargill	Rugby Park (1 other nations test)
New Plymouth	Yarrow Stadium (1 other nations test)
Napier	McLean Park (1 New Zealand test and 1 other)
Palmerston North	The Showgrounds (2 other nations tests)
Rotorua	International Stadium (1 other nations test)
Wellington	Athletic Park (42 New Zealand tests and 3 others) Westpac Stadium (7 New Zealand tests and 1 other)

NOTE: the other nations games were mostly those played during the 1987 World Cup.

Nelson and me

This was one of my most memorable days. I was honoured to meet former South African President Nelson Mandela in Cape Town in 1999. Fellow broadcaster Greg Clark *(on the right in the top photo)* and I wanted an "exclusive" moment with the great man. Careful editing shows that can happen.

Prized tie

I love this story, which came out of a 2006 Rydges Club luncheon in Christchurch. The functions are in worthy support of the Ronald McDonald House Child Charity South Island organisation. At the sold-out lunch the guest speaker was New Zealand Rugby Union chairman Jock Hobbs. The thrust of Jock's address concerned the 2011 World Cup bid in Dublin and New Zealand's success. It was reportedly a very fine speech and the locals said chairman Jock still seemed quite emotional speaking several months after that heady day when New Zealand was awarded the hosting rights.

It is traditional at the Rydges Club that the guest speaker brings something of personal significance to auction for fundraising. Jock had forgotten to do that. However, after gentle persuasion Jock offered his New Zealand Rugby Union 2011 bid tie.

And so the bidding started. The auctioneer, former test cricketer Bryan Andrews, and lunch MC Pete Smith were delighted as the bidding soared past what might normally have been considered "reasonable".

In the end the tie went for nearly $1500. A local man was very happy with his prize. But then the question was asked: who was the other mystery bidder who hung in, thus pushing the bids higher and higher?

Why, it was Jock Hobbs himself. It seems Mr Chairman was desperately trying to buy back his own tie. Those ties are apparently *extremely* rare.

The haka that never was

An impassioned article in a recent edition of the *Sydney Morning Herald* caught my attention. It was part of a series of colourful and heartfelt memories from that lively and always quotable character of Australian rugby, Dave Brockhoff. The former Wallaby recalled facing the All Black haka during his test match days in New Zealand in 1949.

In the story "Brock" remembered the chant of the haka at Athletic Park before the first test. Brockhoff said: "Putting on the damn theatrics of their war cry. I was so savage before that game I was frightened of them… I went mad in the first test minutes… When confronted by the haka on the field I was always moved. It made me want to get stuck into them."

Thinking this had a strange feel to it, I got on the phone to the great Richard "Tiny" White, who lives in Gisborne. He had made his All Black debut in that game. He told me that if Brockhoff was saying the All Blacks did the haka at Wellington in 1949, he was "talking through a hole in his hat".

That's good enough for me. Students of the haka's place in New Zealand know that it was not performed in New Zealand until 1975. Could Brockhoff instead be thinking of the time, earlier in 1949, when he played for Australia against the New Zealand Maori team in Australia? They most certainly would have performed the haka. Or maybe when he played against the All Blacks in Australia in 1951?

Tiny White could not resist a counter-crack at his old rival. "When that 1949 Wallaby team came to Gisborne to play us, I had my feet flipped over in every lineout. I remember it well. Sometimes it looked like I was going to land on my head. It was Brockhoff who did that to me, along with two other Aussie forwards, Nick Shehadie and Rex Mossop. I said to my captain, Ian Shaw, 'We might have to sort this out, Ian. And we did.'"

2006

Preparation the key

While in Adelaide for the 2007 sevens tournament I happened to be on the same hotel floor as the winning Fiji squad. That gave me a unique insight into the depth of preparation the Fiji team undergoes. Check out these two team lists from the final morning and evening of the tournament. The schedules were posted on the door of coach Waisale Serevi's room.

The word "lotu" is the Fijian call to morning prayer (6.30am). Then follows breakfast, strapping, captain's meeting and departure for "the war zone" (the Adelaide Oval).

The insight into the Fijians' work ethic is underscored by the day's biblical quotes of inspiration.

An interpretation of Joshua 14:12 says: "Give me therefore this mountain, which the Lord promised, and if the Lord will be with me, I shall be able to destroy them ..."

> " Joshua 14:12 "
> Mission 20 points
>
> 6:30 AM — Lotu
> 7:00 AM — Breakfast
> 9:00 AM — Strapping
> 10:30 AM — Capt's Meeting
> 10:45 AM — Leave 4 War zone
> 10:55 AM — In the Bus
> 11:27 AM — Warm Up.
>
> ★ Kua Ni Bera Keke²
> ★We train to Play, Play to Win!!!
> ★Tatavulaki ira, Samulaki ira!!!
> ★We can do it, with God nothins impossible!!
> — Phil 4:13 – Take it Home!!!

> "Joshua 14:12"
> – Give me the Mountain –
> Goal 20 points.
>
> 11:00 AM — Strapping
> 11:45 AM — Capt's Meeting
> 11:55 AM – meet at the lift
> 12:00 pm — Bus leaves 4 Warzone
> 1:12 pm — Kickoff Fiji – SA ¼ final
> 3:56 pm — Semifinal Fiji – ?
> 6:20 pm — Final   Fiji – o cei tale!!!
>
> No te –
> ★ Boy's give it all we are fitter, stronger, faster than them + God nothins impossible (Phil 4:13)
> ★Take it Home Boys!!!

With Waisale Serevi, the mastermind of Fijian sevens rugby and instigator of the plans and prayers.

And Philippians 4:13 is the "traditional" inspiration of Fijian sports teams: "I can do all things through Him who strengthens me."

Seeing that Fiji won the sevens tournament in Adelaide, which put them in the lead in the world circuit, should we assume that these examples of belief, commitment and determination are the reasons why?

135

Meteoric rise

While in Melbourne in 2006, a local asked me which New Zealander from the Otahuhu Club, in Auckland, played in the fourth grade one year in Auckland and was in the Wallabies a year later. The answer, it transpires, is Ernie Hills. In 1949 the teenager was in the winning fourth grade team in Auckland. "Nigger" Hills (another nickname that would not pass muster today) was such a fast runner that he decided to head to Victoria to pursue a career in cash sprinting. Turning out in Melbourne club rugby in 1950, he attracted the eye of the Australian rugby selectors. After he'd had only a handful of club games they rushed him into their test team for two matches against the touring British Lions. Hills played tolerably well, but was not required again for Australia. Still, Hills went from fourth grade club rugby to test rugby in different countries within a season, bypassing the rep scene. Ah, the good old days of club rugby.

Clansmen still going strong

In February 2006 I mentioned that the "Edmonton Rugby Club", in Alberta, Canada, was to host matches at the women's World Cup. Working from memory I recalled the time I visited the club ground, Ellerslie, and quoted the club's motto: "Help take violence off the streets and put it back on the rugby field where it belongs."

An alert reader, presumably with strong connections to the current rugby set-up in Edmonton, has emailed to say my information was only partly correct. Michael Sparks tells me that the club's name is actually the Edmonton Clansmen Rugby Club and that the club, established in 1967, is still going strong. Mr Sparks says he still has the infamous business card of years ago, which apart from publishing the above club motto, also boldly claimed that Clansmen members would be useful for "Wars fought, Saloons emptied, Uprisings arranged, Revolutions quelled, Governments run, Orgies organised, Grannies gratified, Virgins converted and Vasectomies verified".

Hyphens abound

It used to be that a hyphenated surname was regarded by some as a sign of elevated social standing. But these days, with many women reluctant to give up their maiden names, there are hyphenated surnames everywhere. Just look at the 2007 Super 14: Adam Ashley-Cooper, Adam Wallace-Harrison, Aaron Broughton-Rouse, Tatafu Polota-Nau, Sam Norton-Knight, Hale T-Pole, Onasai Tololima-Auva'a and, my favourite, a bloke from the Force squad named Tajhon Smallman-Mailata.

Take it from me, this is an alarming trend. I've checked the New Zealand Rugby Almanack from 1996, the first year of professional rugby, and there wasn't a hyphenated name to be seen in any Super 12 team.

NOTE: The last test All Black with a hyphen was Mark Brooke-Cowden, in 1987. According to rumour Mark would have played more, but coach Alex Grizz-Wyllie banned hyphenated names in the All Blacks.

Cockroach costs test place

A great piece of investigative journalism has been carried out by Peter Jackson in London's *Daily Mail*. Apparently former All Black Brad Johnstone, when he was coaching Italy, had to drop a player because the player had a phobia about cockroaches.

Fullback Andrea Scanavacca is back in the Italian team this year after an absence of six years. According to the *Mail*, Johnstone once took Scanavacca on an Italian tour of the South Pacific. Johnstone said: "I never had any doubt about Andrea's kicking ability, but when I took him to the South Pacific the young man found a cockroach in his bedroom. Because of that he couldn't sleep all week and wouldn't practise. So I didn't pick him."

2007

When smoking was the norm

These days, to see an All Black smoking a cigarette is quite rare. Smoking is not outlawed in the All Blacks but it is definitely seen as not good for health or image. However, the 1905-06 All Blacks even endorsed smoking, and only one of the 29 players in the 1924-25 team, one of the greatest All Black teams of all time, was a non-smoker. His name? George Nepia.

The 1905-06 Originals endorsed BDV cigarettes.

Hard to stomach

Worst newspaper headline for a long time goes to the Hong Kong daily newspaper that was reporting a stomach upset among members of the Australian team at the Hong Kong sevens. After the Australians hadn't played too well on the first day, the headline on the sports pages read "Sluggish Aussies call it Squits", followed by "Instead of tries they got the trots".

2001

A hard man with an unforgettable nickname

It was sad to note the death last week of Morrinsville's Keith Arnold. He was one of the hard men of All Black and Kiwi Army teams in the years after World War II and would have had more tests but for the years he was busy fighting for this country. After the conflict he appeared in 25 of the 38 games the famous Kiwis team played on their tour of Europe and New Zealand.

Dripping wet Keith weighed only 12½ stone (80kg), yet he was a rampaging flanker who made life a nightmare for opposing halfbacks. On the 1947 All Black tour of Australia the Aussie half was little Cyril Burke, who was given a torrid time by Arnold. Burke was scragged with such venom that the local radio commentator, Bill Cerrutti, formerly a tough player himself, nicknamed the New Zealander "Killer" Arnold. The tag stuck, though in today's PC world such a name might not be approved of – "Killer" McCaw? I don't think so!

The story I most liked about Arnold concerned his marriage in 1942. He travelled by train from the Waiouru military training camp to Hinuera in Waikato in the middle of the night and got married the next day. He saw his new bride only on his infrequent weekends of leave, then later that year he was sent to Italy, where he fought until the end of the war. He didn't get home until mid-1946. Notwithstanding, Keith and his wife Ada were brilliantly married for more than 60 years.

2006

Vision trouble for refs

Lifted from a recent edition of the official newsletter of the New Zealand Rugby Referees Association:

"Referees are often accused of being blind. Well, scientists have discovered that referees and linesmen actually do have a vision problem.

"Put simply, it takes about 300 milliseconds (a third of a second) for the image of what a referee sees to focus on the tiny spot in the centre of the retina where the picture can register in the brain – the fovea. In that time a player, running at 7.3 metres per second, travels 2.1 metres – more than enough to take them from an on-side position to an offside one."

1999

Buddha the large

Joseph Romanos Collection

The indomitable Chris "Buddha" Handy.

When popular Australian rugby commentator and former Wallaby Chris "Buddha" Handy turned 50, his rugby mates in Brisbane organised a celebrity roast dinner for him. During a great night Chris's burly size assisted those who wanted to make quips and jokes about him.

It is that reported the best one came from former Australian captain Rod McCall, who told the audience: "In his young days Chris was so small they thought he was suffering from anorexia nervosa. Now they think he's got anorexia ponderosa."

2000

Memories of a nightmare

In times of great distress — that's after not winning the World Cup, I suppose — it's always great to hark back to the "good old days". With that in mind, here's a quote I kept where Martin Bayfield, the big England lock, reflected on playing against Frank Bunce in the famous England-New Zealand match at Cape Town in 1995.

Bayfield writes: "There we were, seven minutes gone and we were 12-0 down. The All Blacks were awesome that day. One time Frank Bunce hit me in a tackle and it was the hardest I'd ever been hit. He cut me in half. And as he got up he trod on my ankle, stuck his hand in my face and thrust his fingers up my nose."

The man who said the "b" word

Why the fuss about Toyota using the word "bugger" in a television commercial? You'd think that the word had never played a public role in New Zealand before.

For goodness sake, doesn't anyone remember the epic speech made by the great All Black Peter Jones, after the fourth test against South Africa in Auckland in 1956?

After New Zealand won the game, and therefore the series, the huge crowd chanted for their All Black heroes to come to the public address system and speak to the throng. Peter Jones was one of them. Grasping the microphone in his huge paw, the exhausted Jones said: "I never want to play a game like that again. I'm absolutely buggered."

In the stoic, conservative New Zealand of the 1950s the use of that word resulted in total shock, though in the scratchy Radio New Zealand recording of the speech you can hear a huge roar of delight rise from the crowd. The speech was the talk of the nation.

It ought to be added that a memo was issued that prohibited the recording being played again by Radio New Zealand (NZBC as it was called then). The tape was locked away and was not used again until Dunedin broadcaster Peter Sellers used the word in a special tribute programme in the 1980s.

1999

Can't play, gone shopping

Scottish rugby might be doomed. That's the only conclusion that can be drawn after reading a recent column by John Beattie in the *Glasgow Herald*.

Beattie reported that before Christmas the Helensburgh Rugby Club surprisingly called off one of its regular games. The abandonment was not because of any weather problems, the kind that sometimes affect games in that part of the world.

No. Helensburgh could not field a team for one of its matches "because several of the players were unavailable because they had Christmas shopping to do with their wives and girlfriends".

1998

THE SILVER FERN EMBLEM OF THE ALL BLACKS

The All Mighty All Macs

The Mac Blacks

This really was a team of All Black Macs. Graham Mourie's 1978 All Black team to Britain had 15 players with genuine connections to Scottish clans.

One fine day in Edinburgh they put on the appropriate kilts and posed for this unusual photograph. The All Blacks are *(from left)*: Billy Bush, Andy Dalton, Doug Bruce, Eddie Dunn, John Black, John Fleming, Dave Loveridge, Graham Mourie, Brad Johnstone, Robert Kururangi, Richard Wilson, Stuart Wilson, Brian McKechnie, Barry Ashworth, Ash McGregor.

This item has got me thinking about a team of "All Mac" All Blacks. How about this: Leon MacDonald, Don McKay, Scott McLeod, Luke McAlister, Bruce McPhail, Brian McKechnie, Paul McGahan, Ash McGregor, Richie McCaw, Don McIntosh, Nev MacEwan, Hamish Macdonald, Joe McDonnell, Bruce McLeod, Steve McDowell.

Record maul ruled out

Apparently there is a rugby club in England with the delightful name of Old Mid-Whitgiftians (say it out loud with a plummy accent – and you'll get the drift of what they're like).

OM-W (my abbreviation) made the news when it protested that the *Guinness Book of Records* had declined its request to have one of its team's rolling mauls recognised as a world record. It is claiming that in a recent game an OM-W maul rumbled 50 metres downfield and ended in a try. Oh dear! What a shame we missed that thrilling event in rugby history!

Writing to the *Guinness* book seems to have become the norm for some English clubs. The Surrey club has asked if its team's try, which was scored just 15 seconds after a game kicked off, was a world record. Guinness replied by reminding the club that Leo Price, an England flanker, scored after just 10 seconds of the England-Wales match in 1923.

That brought a howl of protest from the Widden Old Boys Club, which claimed that its dashing winger, Andy Brown, took just eight seconds to score direct from the kick-off in a match against Ashtonians in 1990. It claims to have the incident recorded on video.

2000

Long wait

If you hear any modern All Blacks complaining about tests being played on consecutive weekends, spare a thought for the 1949 All Blacks. Players in that team felt that there was *too much* time between their selection and their first tour game.

The All Black team for that first post-war journey to South Africa played their first tour match in Cape Town on May 31, 1949. The team had been chosen after the final trials on September 18, 1948. The wait from selection to kick-off was therefore eight months and two weeks.

Vote of no-confidence

Mata'afa Keenan told me this one. At the 1991 World Cup in Britain the Samoan team were really fired up before they played Scotland in their quarter-final match in Edinburgh. They had every right to be confident, after their victories over Wales and Argentina.

However, Mata'afa said the team's confidence was deflated somewhat when they boarded their bus to go to the ground. Getting on with them was a local travel agent, who demanded each of the team reach into their bags and hand over their passports.

Apparently he had looked at both teams at their pre-test training and, acting on his instincts, booked the whole Samoa team to fly home the next day. The Samoans could only wonder at this canny Scot, who did not want any team disrupting his World Cup profit margin by staying an extra night after being eliminated from the tournament.

It would be nice to end this story by saying that the Samoans pummeled the Scots. Alas, they did not and, you guessed it, they were on the plane home the very next morning.

To wash or not to wash

This note is from a dusty magazine I read recently. One day on the 1905-06 All Black tour of Britain, Auckland hooker George "Bubs" Tyler went to a reception and shook hands with the King of England, Edward VII, the son of Queen Victoria. Tyler was evidently so honoured and impressed by meeting the great leader that afterwards he chose not to wash his hands for several weeks.

Tyler's unconventional hygiene habits were fair enough, I suppose, given freedom of choice and all that. But it has crossed my mind that during the time that he did not wash his hands Tyler played in several further tour games on the muddy British grounds that existed then. And there would have been all the normal eating, drinking and toilet activities. Plus all those strange places where hookers put their hands during a game of rugby!

Colourful character laid low

Popular former Welsh rugby captain Ray Gravell, aged only 56, has suffered from diabetes for years and has just undergone surgery to have his right leg amputated below the knee. His hospital and home is being swamped with get-well messages.

With Ray Gravell, one of the heroes of Llanelli's never-to-be-forgotten win over the All Blacks.

Gravell, a tough centre, played for Llanelli in 1972 in their famous 9-3 win over the All Blacks, and in the much talked-about test at Cardiff in 1978.

He gave rugby one of its great quotes: *"In any game you've got to get your first tackle in early, even if it's late."*

Away from rugby Ray has had a colourful life. He has been a pop singer, TV and film actor, promoter of the Welsh language and a TV rugby commentator. One time, when he was broadcasting in Argentina, his co-commentator, Wyn Gruffydd, reported that Ray suddenly became agitated, patting his jacket pockets and searching animatedly under his seat. At halftime he announced to Gruffydd: "These locals! They've stolen my wallet!" He was very upset.

This incident took place in the days before cellphones. When the game kicked off in the second half, the first words Ray shouted into the microphones were directed to his wife back home. "Mari," thundered Ray, "cancel the credit cards!" Ray later found his wallet in the side-pocket of the stylish cargo pants he had bought the day before.

2007

Ronald Jorgensen, All Black

Former Wellington representative and New Zealand Junior All Black Neil Sorenson, who has a great sense of humour, tells this story about how he once claimed to be an All Black.

He coached rugby for a time in Singapore. One day he went to a big local soccer match and sat on the terraces with a sports bag over his shoulder on which were New Zealand sports motifs. Soon he was aware of two local youths looking at him and at the bag. One asked: "Are you a New Zealander?" Neil told them he was. After a time came another question: "Are you a rugby player?" Again Neil replied in the affirmative.

Then came the killer question: "Are you an All Black?" Neil looked surrep-titiously around the soccer stadium, thought "what the heck, I'm in Singapore" and said to the lads: "Yes, I am actually." The two youngsters then thrust autograph books into his hands.

Neil says he glanced about sheepishly and carefully signed: "Best wishes, Ronald Jorgensen."

1997

The unluckiest non-All Black

A few years ago in a pub in Dunedin Peter Sellers, the veteran radio broadcaster and a good friend, pointed out an elderly man sitting quietly in a corner with his glass of beer. Peter made the statement that "that bloke over there is probably the unluckiest player never to be an All Black".

The old bloke's name turned out to be L K "Toucher" Heazlewood, and after hearing of his record few would dispute Peter Sellers' assertion. Through the 1920s and 30s Heazlewood, mainly a fullback, played representative rugby for Auckland, Wellington, Canterbury and Otago. He also played for the South Island (1927) and the North Island (1930) and had no fewer than five All Black trials. But he was never chosen for the All Blacks.

It must be very doubtful if anyone could match Heazlewood's record of excellence and achievement, without recognition at the top level.

Rugby network rules

You can never beat the rugby network that exists among decent, honorable New Zealanders. Here's an example of why.

A few years ago the New Zealand Rugby Museum in Palmerston North was burgled. Among the items stolen was one of museum's most prized possessions, the 1931-38 Springbok blazer of the great Danie Craven.

It was a distinctive garment, with the dates of the years Craven had played for his country lovingly embroidered in gold lettering on its green material. The burglar obviously realised that he had something of worth in his haul and put the word out in the little town of Waikanae, north of Wellington, that he wanted to make a sale.

A local collector of sports memorabilia became interested in a purchase but, understandably, wondered about paying a high price for the blazer without checking its authenticity. Where better to check with than the New Zealand Rugby Museum?

Well, you know the answer to this one already. The museum curator said: "Oh really?" when he heard that Craven's blazer was for sale somewhere. A couple of calls later and the police were on their way to Waikanae, where they arrested the seller.

The Craven blazer was returned to the Rugby Museum, where it went back on display.

1997

Pickles White?

Is this a true story or is a famous All Black having me on? The 1953-55 All Black H L ("Snow") White has the Christian names of Hallard Leo. I asked him about these one day and, in all seriousness, "Snow" told me that his first name was settled on when his mother saw it on the label of a well-known brand of pickles.

Give that man a canary

Now, a classic story that many rugby players might identify with from their touring days.

In his excellent book *From the Ruck*, Australian television commentator Gordon Bray writes that while the Wallaby team was touring New Zealand in 1962, big Sydney forward Dick Thornett complained of regular "stomach pains". Bray reports that it got so embarrassing for Thornett that at one point the team bus-driver was commanded to pull over to the side of the road. Thornett's team-mates then tumbled on to the roadside for relief from the odours!

At a reunion years later the popular Thornett had been forgiven, but the incident had not been forgotten. His mates from that tour presented him with a cage with a canary in it. It was, they said, for him to hang in his bar, in case he was ever again stricken by the "distressing ailment" of his 1962 tour.

Some of the great kicks

In the recent discussions about a proposed new ball, which might or might not produce regular successful goal-kicks from 70 metres, it is worth noting that such kicks have occasionally been achieved with the old leather balls.

The gigantic goal-kick that French fullback Pierre Villepreux landed at Athletic Park in Wellington was calculated by reporters at the time to be of 68 metres.

Also in the mists of time, there was another kick at Athletic Park that was even longer. In 1985, in an NPC game between Wellington and Manawatu, up stepped Wellington's Evan Hopkin. The 24-year-old fullback placed the ball 10 metres from the eastern touchline and one metre "outside" his own 10-metre line. The kick was 70 metres.

One touch judge, Craig Reilly, said the ball "sailed about four or five metres above the crossbar".

The clipping (next page) confirms that Hopkins' kick was probably the longest seen on Athletic Park. Wellington won the game 28-9.

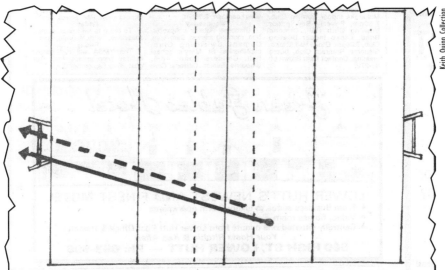

A COMPARISON between Frenchman Pierre Villepreux's kick in 1968 (dotted line) and Evan Hopkin's bigger effort last Saturday at Athletic Park.

Hopkin lands big kick

By IAN GAULT

EVAN HOPKIN kicked what is believed to be the biggest penalty goal seen on Athletic Park when Wellington beat Manawatu 28-9 in a national championship first division rugby match on Saturday.

Hopkin, 24, placed the ball 10 metres in from the eastern touchline and one metre outside his own 10 metre line, a distance of about 70 metres.

"I hit it dead smack in the middle and it felt good, but I wondered if it had enough to get there," said Hopkin.

"I didn't allow much for the ball sailed about four or five

HOPKIN . . . felt good

"I remember landing a penalty against Marist-St Pats in 1982 which was about 65 metres and one of about that distance at the Polo Ground in 1984," he said.

In the second test of the 1968 tour by France, fullback Pierre Villepreux caused pandemonium when he slotted a penalty from 15 metres in from the eastern touch and about three metres inside his own 10 metre line — roughly the same angle as Hopkin, but shorter.

After missing the first six games of the Wellington club season because he was playing

The *Herald on Sunday* also said the other day that the great Don Clarke kicked a 69-metre goal in a charity game in Te Kuiti. However, that kick was made during an exhibition at halftime and therefore not under match conditions.

I have a clipping from the 1962 All Black tour of Australia. It is headlined "Don Clarke kicks 85-yarder". It was a placekick aimed only for distance and not for goal, and was achieved in an exhibition with two local AFL kickers before the All Blacks' game against Victoria.

2004

Don't try to be Clive, Robbo

Having lost their acclaimed coach, their World Cup-winning captain, their stand-in captain, an entire generation of test players and five of their last six tests, there is no doubt that England have a very tough road ahead, no-one more so than new coach Andy Robinson.

Not only does Robinson have to consider all of the above, but he is getting advice from all quarters as well.

Take this recent comment in *The Independent*, when writer Chris Hewett set out the "First Fifteen" problems Robinson has to surmount before he can "make England great again".

1 Do not try to be Sir Clive Woodward. Be yourself, Robbo.
2. The search must be a priority to a find at least one big, aggressive, horrible forward in the Martin Johnson mould.
3. Form a good relationship with the Premiership clubs around England.
4. Bring back into the fold Brian Ashton, "the most imaginative coach in Europe".
5. Defy medical science. Get back free from seemingly permanent injury players like Wilkinson, Vickery, Moody, Lewsey and Simon Shaw.
6. Get your backline players to rediscover the art of passing.
7. Rise above the Lions. England will contribute a large number of players to that team. They will come home from New Zealand tired and stressed.
8. Combat the renaissance of South African rugby. We already know England are drawn to play them in the pool play of the 2007 World Cup.
9. Keep the Celtic nations in their places. Win well in Dublin and Cardiff in this upcoming Six Nations season.
10. Learn the art of coaching out-of-form top players back to their best.
11. Name two of Jonny Wilkinson, Charlie Hodgson or Ollie Barkley in the same team. They are all top-class fly-halves and brilliant players. They must all be kept happy.
12. Avoid rugby politics at all times.
13. Learn how to cope with losing. Defeats may come thick and fast.

14. Learn how to cope with being English. The English team was invented so rugby people of other nations could be united in their aversion to public-school twits. Times have changed but the antipathy lingers. Deal with it.
15. Keep your eyes on the ball. Do not ever lose concentration on the job at hand.

2004

The Great Auk back in the news

I wonder if any other "old timers" caught this news on television and had a moment of nostalgic reflection. Fox TV UK ran a story that someone had been questioning the whereabouts of a giant ocean bird called the Great Auk. The news item, which I only half-heard, also contained a reference to a bird called The Great Bustard.

Whether these two fine creatures still exist is of no importance to me here. What the mention of them did trigger was the memory of when the Auckland Rugby Union went looking for a mascot for its rep team. The Aucklanders were about to challenge Wellington for the Ranfurly Shield. This was way back in 1957, but I can remember as a boy going to Athletic Park and being frightened by a creature called The Great Auk, the Auckland mascot.

It was like a giant stuffed blue-and-white penguin and it waddled about in a ponderous manner. The crowd hooted and hollered at it. It couldn't do anything except walk and stop. It was obvious, even to we boys, that there was a man inside, because there was a sizable slot across the bird's breast and we could see a pair of eyes peering out. A couple of my mates attempted to tackle it.

I guess I recall this only because I grew to hate that creature. Auckland won the shield that day – the Great Auk had flown in successfully, you might say. I think Auckland had one more home game that season and when the ridiculous bird appeared on Eden Park the locals laughed at him too.

As he was never seen again after that year, can anyone help an aging, self-appointed historian? What was the story behind the Great Auk? And why not, seeing he's in the news again, bring him back?

2004

A kamikaze failure

With the great Japanese rugby man, Shiggy Konno.

Japanese rugby supremo **Shiggy Konno** was one of the great figures of the game, an official from outside the heavyweight rugby nations (at least in terms of test performances) who was able to rub shoulders with all the big-wigs on the International Rugby Board. He was extremely popular and thought deeply about the game, so his views were valued.

When I heard about **Shiggy's** death in 2007 any number of memories of his ever-smiling face and cheerful personality

continued next page

flooded back. He fought for years to establish the game he loved in Japan and, looking back, you'd have to say he did an outstanding job in the face of what must have seemed in the early days like overwhelming odds.

However, there was one story that he told me that was particularly poignant and there was no sparkle in his eyes when he related it. It concerned Shiggy's time fighting for Japan during World War II.

He described himself as a "failed kamikaze pilot" and explained: "It was like this. I was in the Japanese Air Force in the Pacific and things were looking gloomy for us. Before a battle we pilots were taken into a room on our aircraft carrier.

"We were told grimly we would all have to volunteer to take part in the next 'special' operation. The word 'kamikaze' was used to us. We all knew what that meant [to fly a no-return death mission]. So when our commander asked for volunteers to 'give our lives for the Emperor', we all of course instantly put our hands up for selection."

Shiggy then recalled that he was one of those not chosen to fly that day. "Those of us left living considered we had therefore not been good enough. We felt we had 'failed' our Emperor."

After the interview we were then shown precious Japanese archive footage of the pilots departing on their final mission. As each plane took off, those not chosen stood dramatically along the carrier's deck, waving white silk scarves in farewell. As he told me that story, the normally dignified and always composed Shiggy's eyes welled up with tears.

Shiggy was chairman of the Japan Rugby Union from 1972-94 and managed the Japanese team at the 1987 and 1991 World Cups. When Japan was given full council status on the world governing body, he became their IRB representative from 1991-2000.

He also made a lifetime commitment to improving relations between Japan and Britain, and his trade relations and sports links earned him an honorary OBE.

Lurch was never a Lion

Which rugby international from the four home unions played the most test matches but never went on a Lions tour? Some clues for you: his career spanned five Lions tours; he was Welsh; and he eventually played 92 tests.

The answer: Gareth Llewellyn. From 1989, when the giant lock marked Gary Whetton in the New Zealand-Wales match on his debut, to his final test last northern winter, "Lurch" was never invited to be a Lion.

 2005

An own try

The co-editor of the *New Zealand Rugby Almanack*, Clive Akers, sent me an unusual story about another member of the famous Belliss family.

The story concerned an own score, not in soccer, but – believe it or not – rugby. Apparently Jack Belliss is the only New Zealand first-class rugby player to have scored for the opposition.

Belliss was in the Wanganui team that played Manawatu in 1941. A ball was kicked over his team's goal-line and Belliss forced it behind his goalpost. Of course, he anticipated a drop-out restart from the 22-metre line (the 25-yard line in those days).

But the ref awarded a try in error to Manawatu. It is not recorded whether there was a stream of protest from the Wanganui players. At the very least, they were no doubt highly confused. The conversion sailed between the posts.

Manawatu won the game 8-3, so the converted try was the difference. Clive Akers reports that the 1941 season's records officially show E V ("Jack") Belliss (Wanganui) listed among the Manawatu points-scorers.

 2006

An extra "y" saves the day

It's never too late to hear hard-case stories about what really occurred on rugby tours. In a social meeting (late afternoon, King's Seat Hotel, in Dollar, Scotland) I was introduced to Adam Buchanan-Smith, whose name and face I recognised from the 1991 Scotland tour of New Zealand.

Surrounded by local luminaries, Adam spoke with fond memories of his time in New Zealand, talking of the passion he found for the game. "Why," he said, "on the morning of the Wellington game my roommate Doug Wylie and I were lying on our beds and two blokes came on the radio wildly rubbishing us as players. I was described as just an average club player and Doug, it was said by these blokes, was so hopeless he could only pass one way. We couldn't get over how our play could be analysed so closely."

I gulped. I think Phil Gifford and I were in full flight in those days on the *Radio Rugby Show* and we were the broadcasters this man was referring to.

Adam also recalled a great internal drama concerning the sale of Scottish team T-shirts in those amateur days. Before they left for the tour, some of the senior Scottish players had T-shirts printed to sell to the New Zealand public. There were boxes and boxes of them and they would be a good fund-raiser for the team.

On the front of the shirt was a giant Scottish claymore-wielding warrior, à la *Braveheart*. On the back were printed the autographs of all of the team members. But with 30 players in the squad, plus a couple of officials, the names did not fit into three equal columns. To balance the columns, one hard-case player added in the name R S Hole (get it?).

It became a team joke. But the manager, Duncan Paterson, didn't feel the joke was in keeping with the dignity of the team and the tour, and banned the sale of the T-shirts. The players were disappointed – a lot of money would be lost.

However, Buchanan-Smith reported to me that back then the Scottish lads were nothing if not resourceful. Some younger members of the team were sent out to buy several felt-tipped pens and one evening, for hours, they added one letter to R S Hole's signature.

So if you keep old touring memorabilia check to see if you have that T-shirt from 1991. If you have, look for the name "R S Holey" at the bottom of one column. The extra "Y" saved the day, and a sound investment for the Scottish touring team was saved.

2004

A kilt and a jockstrap

Another Scottish story concerns a man named Peter Kirkwood, also of Dollar. Peter is a great guy, with a rich fund of rugby stories.

I like the story about Peter himself best. After his representative career, which included playing for North and Midlands against South Africa in 1969, he turned out in social rugby for the Forth Valley Fossils team against Irish club Kilkenny.

Peter and his mates had a few drinks before the game. Thus fortified, Peter decided he would play the game in his kilt. And he did. He thinks he might not have been the first Scotsman to appear in this "exposed" garb, but suggests he might have been the first to do so on a very muddy field where, as the game wore on, his kilt became heavier and heavier and therefore much harder to run in.

When asked if he played the game "as a true Scotsman" (that is, wearing no underwear, as Scotsmen are supposed to do in everyday life), Peter said: "No, I did concede in that regard. I did wear my favourite old jockstrap."

2004

Perfect record

A Scottish international might play 50 tests, but I've found that the games he is best remembered for are those when he was on the winning side against England. The "auld enemy" is still deeply spurned in Scotland in every conversation about sport.

That makes the international career of Quinton Dunlop one that Scottish trivia lovers recall with relish. You see, Dunlop was part of winning Scottish teams every time he played England.

He was a hooker in the team that in March 1971 travelled to Twickenham and scored a 16-15 win, Scotland's first victory on the ground for 33 years. That was a Five Nations game. A week later Dunlop was retained for the special celebration game staged to mark the centenary of the first rugby international – Scotland v England in 1871.

In front of 75,000 at Murrayfield, in Edinburgh, Scotland won again, this time 26-6. Two wins over England in a week – it was unheard of. The partying would have been long and hard. If Quinton Dunlop could have foreseen the future, he might have partied hardest. You see, he never played for Scotland again.

2004

What chance the Olympics?

On the first day of the 2005 World Cup sevens tournament in Hong Kong, several members of the International Olympic Committee mooched about the Hong Kong stadium. They were in town to gauge whether sevens rugby might be suitable for inclusion in the 2012 Olympic Games. One of these gentlemen, whose job it was to check television facilities, arrived in our broadcast box. He spoke with a strong South African accent, but when he looked at the rugby he said: "What's that called when the men pack down against each other?"

"It's a scrum, sir," we said, as helpfully as we could be.

On that basis, what chance has sevens got of cracking the Olympic big-time?

The excellent tournament programme asked a swag of questions on a quiz page. One of them intrigued to me. It read: "Name the only three players who have won winner's medals at both sevens and fifteens World Cups?"

THE ANSWER: Joost van der Westhuizen, Lawrence Dallaglio and Matt Dawson.

The bowler who wanted more

While at the 2006 Commonwealth Games in Melbourne I met New Zealand bowls legend Peter Belliss, who was at the games as coach of the New Zealand team. Our chat inevitably drifted to rugby. The Belliss name has been synonymous with the game for decades.

Peter's grandfather was the leg-endary "Moke" Belliss, an All Black from 1920-23, and the captain in 1922 against New South Wales.

Peter spoke proudly of his father, Ernest (Jack) Belliss, and Jack's 16-year first-class rugby career. Jack played for Auckland as a No 8 in 1937, but was injured so didn't play the following year. By 1939 he was back in Wanganui, and donned that province's blue and black colours.

Peter Belliss — football representative and handy lawn bowler.

After war service in the Pacific Jack returned to rep rugby as a vigorous prop. He was 37 when he played his last game, in 1953.

Peter is known as a brilliant lawn bowler. When I asked him about his own rugby days he looked off, slightly ruefully, into the afternoon sun. "Yes, it's true that I kept the family name going for good old Wanganui," he said. "I did have four games in 1973 and another four in 1977, but in the time-honoured way of so many of us who feel the selectors could have seen it differently, I definitely feel I should have had a lot more."

A useful man in 15s

This from Eric Rush in the 2006 Hong Kong sevens programme. Rush was asked if he regretted being known as a sevens specialist in his playing days.

His reply: "I don't mind. After all, being a sevens specialist has allowed me to mix with some of the most talented rugby players in the world – Jonah, Christian Cullen, Serevi and Campese. But it was also a pleasure to play with the likes of Karl Tenana and Glen Osborne… Not everyone can be good at both 15-a-side rugby and sevens. I made 29 appearances for the All Blacks, including nine tests, so I could play a bit in the other game too, you know.

Eric Rush – more than useful.

"Remember, I was fighting for my test position with the likes of Va'aiga Tuigamala, John Kirwan, Jeff Wilson and Jonah Lomu. Every New Zealand male dreams of playing for the All Blacks and I achieved that. So I have no qualms about being known as a sevens specialist, but am happy that I was useful in 15s."

Eric Rush useful in fifteens? I'll say he was. Those who saw his thrilling try in the corner against France at the Parc des Princes in Paris in 1995 won't easily forget his talent and dynamic speed.

And another quote from Rush: "When I first saw Jonah, as an 18-year-old at the 1994 Hong Kong sevens, he had a man's body, but we thought he was a bit young. Especially when we saw that he had gone out and bought a remote-controlled car and played with it in the hotel corridors all week."

Entertaining, but...

The success of the 2006 Commonwealth Games sevens tournament has prompted discussion in sports-mad Melbourne. Some are calling for Melbourne to bid for inclusion on to the IRB's world sevens circuit.

While that idea would probably be worth considering, it seems that sevens rugby still has a way to go to gain wide public acceptance in Australia. A survey of nearly 4000 replies on *The Age's* website produced a revealing result:

QUESTION: is sevens the best entertainment rugby provides?

Best entertainment: 24%

Mildly diverting: 20%

A great party, but not really rugby: 52%

An insult to our great game: 4%

Retrospective contracts?

Heard a good line from Colin Meads once. Meads, whose 55 test appearances stood as the New Zealand record for 20 years, felt that perhaps it was time for rugby to investigate a Treaty of Waitangi equivalent.

He suggested innocently that, with all the money now being paid for test and Super 12 rugby, the Rugby Union might look at some retrospective contracts for former All Blacks.

Meads, who also set records by playing 361 first-class matches and 133 matches for New Zealand, would be a millionaire many times over if he was playing now. After all, his international career stretched over 15 years.

What makes his suggestion all the more humorous is that he, of all All Blacks, was the least concerned with being paid. As Fergie McCormick once said: "The All Black jersey was like pure gold for Meads."

2006

Ballboy shows form

The biggest crowd to attend a test match in Wellington. In 1959 it was estimated 58,000 saw the Lions lose to New Zealand in the second test. Recognise the young ball boy running along the touchline, gathering stories for his first edition of *Quinn's Quirks*?

The Hall of Shame

New Zealanders figure strongly in the Sydney *Sun-Herald's* rugby Hall of Shame. The paper has listed the five dirtiest moments in rugby.

Top spot goes to the ear-biting of London Scottish player Simon Fenn by Bath's Kevin Yates in January. Finn required 26 stitches. Second is Johan Le Roux's ear-biting of Sean Fitzpatrick, which earned Le Roux a 19-month suspension from rugby. Third is Colin Meads pulling Ken Catchpole from a ruck and effectively ending the Wallaby halfback's career when he ripped his groin muscle from the bone. Richard Loe earns fourth and fifth positions, for his eye-gouging of Greg Cooper and his attack on Paul Carozza, when he smashed Carozza's nose with his forearm after the Australian had scored for the Wallabies. The New Zealand Rugby Union cleared Loe of all charges on that one.

I repeat the *Sun-Herald's* list only as a talking-point. It is neither fair nor comprehensive. Most incredible is the omission of any Aussie "hard men". A prime candidate would be Steve Finnane, the 1970s prop. His king-hit from behind of Welsh prop Graham Price, at the Sydney Cricket Ground in 1978, forced Price to leave the field with his jaw broken and blood pouring out of his mouth. Finnane used the same cowardly tactics in 1977, when he belted Auckland prop Alan Craig from behind, causing Craig to leave the field with concussion. Off the field Finnane was a well-spoken chap, a solicitor by occupation. But once he walked on to the paddock, any respect for the laws of the game vanished. Ironically, he wrote a book called *The Game They Play in Heaven*.

Meads was involved in some unsavoury incidents, but in the two for which he is most often vilified — the Catchpole affair and his sending off in the Scotland test in 1967 — he was relatively blameless. In the first, he was legitimately trying to clear Catchpole from a ruck and could not have known Catchpole's other leg was trapped. In the second, he was sent off for an innocent kick at a loose ball.

One incident that would have caused a sensation today, with the multi-angled video replays, was the savage kicking in the back of All Black lock Tiny White by Springbok forward Jaap Bekker at Eden Park in 1956. White had to be assisted from the field and never played for New Zealand again.

1998

You can't handle the truth

You'll remember Jack Nicholson's memorable, Academy Award-nominated performance as Colonel Nathan R Jessep, of Guantanamo Bay, in the film A Few Good Men. The highlight of the movie is when Nicholson, in the witness box, is being questioned by Lieutenant Kaffee (Tom Cruise).

Well, former Wallaby lock Peter FitzSimons, now an outstanding journalist and public speaker, has adapted Nicholson's witness box outpouring to rugby. He sets the scene by describing a "thermometer-thin" winger approaching a gnarled prop in the bar and chastising him for constantly starting brawls on the field.

Jack Nicholson — could he play at prop?

The prop's response really demands a Nicholson (or FitzSimons) performance:

"Son," he thunders, "we play in a game that has brawls and those brawls are fought by men called thugs. Who's going to do it? You? I live with a greater responsibility than you can possibly fathom.

"You weep for your wingers and centres and you curse the thug forward. You have that luxury. You have the luxury of not knowing what I know — that my existence, while grotesque and incomprehensible to you, wins these games we play. You can't handle the truth because deep down in places you don't talk about in your wingers' knitting classes, you want me in that brawl. You *need* me in that brawl.

"We use words like 'head-butt', 'eye-gouge' and 'Christmas grip'. We use these words as a backbone to a game spent defending something. You use them as a punch-line.

"I have neither the time nor the interest to explain myself to a namby-pamby winger who scores on and off the field under the very blanket of biffo that I provide and then questions the very manner in which I provide it. I would rather you just bought me a beer and a pie with sauce and went on your way."

1999

Former adversaries Bob Scott and Okey Geffin met again a quarter of century later, for Bob's farewell from the Petone club. Naturally there was a kicking exhibition. Here Bob kicks barefooted, while Geffin holds the ball for him. Watching in disbelief is Fergie McCormick.

We're at war

Okey Geffin, who kicked South Africa to victory in the 1949 series against the All Blacks, once told me about the team talk former Springbok great Boy Louw gave his countrymen just before the first test of that series. Louw looked around at the Springbok players and said solemnly: "For the benefit of my English-speaking friends, we're at war. I want you to remember that I played against their grandfathers and if you can't bite, punch and kick, don't go on the field, because they'll murder you. I want you to play hard and clean, but always remember that it's easier to play against 14 than it is against 15."

Cover blown, out of tour

I was intrigued to discover from Fred Allen one day why brilliant halfback Vince Bevan was not chosen for the 1949 All Black tour of South Africa. Fred, who captained the team, explained: "Vince was an extra good halfback, but he was ruled out after [commentator] Winston McCarthy blew his cover in Newcastle, New South Wales, in 1947.

"Winston mentioned several times during his broadcast that day that we were fielding an all-Maori backline for the first time. Most people didn't know until then that Vince was a Maori because he didn't look like a Maori. But after that there was a big hue and cry in South Africa and he was barred from being selected for the tour. In those days they wouldn't allow us to take over any dark-skinned players.

"The irony was that Maori people didn't feel Vince had enough Maori blood in him to play for the New Zealand Maori team."

Nothing wrong with our knowledge

Talking to overseas players who have toured New Zealand, a recurring theme is how amazed they are at the knowledge of rugby here.

Here's one example, from long-serving England captain Will Carling, who toured New Zealand with the British Lions in 1993: "It was amazing to experience rugby life in New Zealand. We went to the Bay of Islands when we arrived. I went into a chemist on the first morning to buy a tube of toothpaste. There was a lady of about 70 behind the counter who said, 'Are you with the Lions?' I said we were and she went through the squad. She thought our loosies were a bit slow, our wingers were quick etc. Unbelievable! She analysed our whole team, and was spot on.

"It was like that throughout New Zealand. You can't get away from rugby in New Zealand."

1999

Referee and plane-spotter

Not surprisingly, Clive Norling described the third test of the 1981 New Zealand-South Africa series as the most remarkable game of rugby he ever refereed, with the barbed wire, the plane buzzing overhead and the flour bombs.

Talking to Clive years later, it seemed the plane claimed much of his attention. "I had to act as not only referee, but aircraft spotter as well," he said. "After the game Andy Haden told me I'd caused him great problems at one lineout. He said Andy Dalton had signalled for him to jump for the ball just as I'd said, 'Oh, God, boys, here he comes again! Duck, duck, whatever you do, duck!'"

Who is this Buck?

Even now, nearly two decades after Wayne "Buck" Shelford played his last test, you still see "Bring Back Buck" signs at sports events all around the world. I've seen them at Olympic and Commonwealth Games, and even during the last soccer World Cup.

In the early days they were a plea by Shelford's supporters for him to be reinstated to the All Blacks. He had never lost a test as captain when he was sensationally dropped during the series against Australia in 1990. But as time passed the signs have become more a humorous way of New Zealanders signalling their presence at major events, a special code from one group of New Zealanders to their countrymen.

I once asked Shelford about the signs and he told me that a group of university players in Manawatu were the first to fly "Bring Back Buck" banners. "They did it for a laugh," he said, "but it has carried on. It's probably wearing a bit thin now, but probably the people might have been right. There was a dirty thing done, and to the wrong person.

"I've seen the signs in Jamaica, Japan, England, South Africa, Australia, Hong Kong, even at soccer matches in England. People look at the signs and say, 'Who is this Buck?' But it's a good laugh."

1999

Providing leadership

Graham Mourie's decision not to play against the touring Springboks in 1981 was possibly the most significant taken by any New Zealand sportsman of my time. After all, he was the All Black captain, and this *was* a tour by New Zealand's fiercest test rivals, South Africa.

I once asked him to explain his reasons for his decision and he replied with calm logic: "The South African issue had always been a major one for New Zealand rugby, but had become much more important by 1981. I looked at what happened when the Springboks toured Britain in 1969-70 and Australia a year later.

"It seemed to me that a tour of New Zealand by the Springboks would not be good for rugby, or for New Zealand society. And I had a basic belief that sport shouldn't be subject to legislation in terms of whether people would be allowed to play for their countries. Those three issues made it very difficult for me to play against them happily.

"Had we been going to South Africa, I may have been available, because there would have been just one issue. Having the South Africans touring New Zealand created problems within New Zealand. Had I been selected in 1976 I would probably have toured South Africa.

"Another factor was that as captain of the All Blacks I felt there was a leadership issue, and that leaders should make judgments on right and wrong, rather than leading where they thought the team wanted to go without considering the issues."

1999

Kirton the talent-spotter

I've always enjoyed Earle Kirton's company, though not so much in more recent times, when he's been my dentist.

Earle made his All Black debut on the 1963-64 tour of Britain. It wasn't the happiest of tours for him, because the All Blacks lost one game on the tour, to Newport, and some seemed to hold the junior member of the team, Kirton, primarily responsible. He had a tough time marking brilliant Welsh and Lions first-five Dai Watkins and struggled to get games on tour afterwards.

However, as he told me one day, he certainly remembers his next outing after the Newport setback. "I was told I'd have to wait for my next game because they realised I could be a gi-normous liability," said Earle. "So I waited four more games before I got picked again, against Cambridge University.

"This was all right. We had a fairly heavy pack, and Don Clarke was at fullback, and it wasn't a bad day, so I thought I'd get a fair bit of confidence back.

"For a while it was all right, then, early in the second half, I raced after my opposite number and just couldn't get near him. Only a stiff-armed coat-hanger from Don Clarke stopped him from scoring. So I thought I'd go a bit wider on him and come back at him on the angle, but he did me again, beat me hands down. I got beaten three times by this chap.

"Later, I found out his name was Michael Gibson. So within two games I'd played against the two best first-fives Britain had produced in probably 20 years. Gibson was still playing at 40, but they never knew he was any good until he played against me and I showed them. After I finished with him, he was playing for Ireland and the Lions."

Back seat memory

Former All Black captain Andy Dalton once spoke of the back seat of the bus being the spoke of the wheel of the All Blacks.

"The senior players sitting there make the rules – what they say goes," Andy said. "I've a vivid memory of being summoned down to the back seat in 1977 by Bryan Williams, Bruce Robertson, Andy Haden and Brad Johnstone, and being made to stand in front of them. Bryan Williams, who was the senior counsel, asked me what it meant to me to be an All Black. I had to state what my feelings were for the jersey, and to do it to people who were icons of the game and who, except for Bruce Robertson, a Counties team-mate, I didn't know. That was something I'll never forget. It had quite an influence on me."

1999

An artist or a player?

Former All fullback Kit Fawcett always was an original, as this tale from his breakthrough into the top level shows:

"I got picked for the All Black trial in 1974 as an 18-year-old student," he said. "I was in Dunedin, but had not played for Otago, so I didn't have a uniform. My air tickets arrived by mail and I turned up at the hotel.

"They said, 'Who are you?' They asked me where my blazer was. I was wearing a bright red pair of striped leather shoes, and a pink pair of trousers and quite a bright shirt. I think I was wearing a cap, and, of course, I had long hair. They didn't know if I was an artist or what, but they certainly got a shock when I turned up."

1999

I caught up with the much-talked-about and ever-friendly Kit Fawcett and his children in 1999.

Keith Quinn Collection

"Am I boring you, Meads?"

Fred Allen is still regarded as the doyen of All Black coaches, and so he should be. He coached the All Blacks for three years — from 1966-68 — and they never lost. I sometimes wonder how Fred, aptly nicknamed "the Needle", would get on in today's more politically correct, inclusive world. I think he'd do just fine.

Fred used to rule by fear and no players were immune. And he was always looking for ways to spark his team. Here are a couple of examples.

The first occurred during the middle of Auckland's long Ranfurly Shield reign in the early 1960s. "We used to have our team talk in the commercial room in the old Station Hotel," said Fred. "We always used to have the shield there for our final team talk, but on one occasion it wasn't in the room. Barry Thomas asked me where it was and I said I'd lent it to Canterbury, because they wanted a photograph of it with their team, so they could have it ready for the Christchurch papers first thing next morning. After that you really didn't need a team talk. The players were steaming to get out there.

"I'd use any trick to grab their attention. Colin Meads was one of the greatest forwards I ever saw. I had two young fellows in one of my All Black teams and I was looking for a way of getting to them without them being too upset or excited.

"We're having the team talk in the Clarendon Hotel, and everyone's around, very attentive. Then old Pinetree lifts his head and yawns. I said, 'Am I boring you, Meads?' Poor old Pinetree jumped up. 'No, no,' he said. Well, if you'd seen these young lads — that was just the lift they needed. They thought, 'God, if Meads is copping it, what will I get?'"

Fred Allen — fearsome.

How not to prepare for a test debug

How's this for the wrong way to begin your first test! Fullback Robbie Deans made his test debut at Murrayfield, Edinburgh, in 1983, and looked his usual calm, composed self on the field, which was amazing, really, considering what had gone on beforehand.

"We had our team talk and from there it's straight on to the team bus," Deans recalled. "Through some circumstances I don't want to go into, because it'll get me angry, I missed the bus. I arrived at the front door as the bus was pulling out, which was fairly traumatic, though at least it got my mind off first-test nerves.

"I got a taxi and was heading to the ground. Then the guys on the bus realised I wasn't on board and turned the bus around. They passed me going the other way, back to the hotel. I got stuck in traffic heading towards the ground, whereas they had a police escort.

"When I finally arrived at Murrayfield, I had to convince the man on the gate that I was playing. Obviously others had tried to have him on, because he took some convincing!"

Revenge at last

I love this summary of Colin Meads by John Gainsford, the fine Springbok centre of the 1960s: "Colin Meads was the greatest player I played against. He was a character as a player. Everything about him was magnificent and I loved him as a man, still do, even if he did remove my front teeth at Newlands in the second test in 1960. Meads had an aura and respect about him, but also a wonderful sense of humour.

"After we played the first test in 1965, we went down to play King Country and the combined provinces. He tackled me during the game and grabbed hold of me and squeezed me where it hurts a little bit. He said he'd been trying to get me for a couple of days and gave me a little tug.

"At the end of the game, which they won, I went up to him and told him I hadn't been able to repay him during the game, but that I was going to give him something that nobody could send me off the field for. I grabbed a handful of mud and rubbed it into his face as hard as I could!"

1999

George's tribute

Another verb has entered rugby terminology. From Canberra, the Brumbies' George Gregan, when asked to comment on Steve Larkham's winning dropped goal against the Crusaders, said: "He didn't hit the kick hard. In fact, he just Serevi'd it over…"

As someone who has seen Waisale Serevi kick a million conversions for Fiji over the years I know exactly what Gregan meant.

Lest we forget

Concerning rugby and Anzac Day, well done to Clive Akers, editor of the *New Zealand Rugby Almanack*. These days our top professional players would have hardly any concept of wartime camaraderie. So it's worth remembering the sacrifices others made along the way to allow us to enjoy today's peaceful times.

Many fine New Zealand rugby players were killed doing war service – 20 All Blacks died in action in the two world wars. Thousands of other provincial players also served.

Akers has now written about the Bonar brothers, Archibald and Hugh, who played rugby at Nelson College and then for Nelson province (Archie also played for Wellington.) Tragically, these fine young sportsmen lost their lives at Gallipoli.

Both brothers had served in the Boer War (1899-1902) and, just when they might have thought that their futures would have revolved around family and civilian life, they were called for duty again.

They were among the first New Zealanders to arrive at Gallipoli, on April 25, 1915.

Their time on land was to be tragically brief. They were pitched into a day of constant attack from the Turkish forces. Archie was killed shortly after midnight on April 26. He had been ashore for less than 24 hours.

Hugh lasted 13 more days, and then died at a place that became known as the "Daisy Patch".

Akers writes: "It was a wide field covered in pretty flowers. On May 8 the New Zealanders were ordered to charge across the exposed area by their British commanding officers. 'It was suicide,' one survivor recalled. 'Our path was like a golf fairway... [Our men] were mown down by Turkish machine guns.'

"In all, 170 New Zealanders died on the "Daisy Patch" that day, Hugh Bonar being one of them."

Archibald and Hugh Bonar were not famous New Zealand rugby players. Indeed, you could say they were modest rugby achievers. But they were two of five brothers from a sports-loving South Island family who believed in serving their country. To me they are heroes.

Many New Zealand families lost sons in the wars. Two brothers dying within a fortnight was just one example of the high cost the people of that time made. On days like Anzac Day we should reflect on the Bonars and all the others who gave their lives for the freedom we enjoy today.

Early tip for the All Blacks

About four years ago I was accepted as a full member of the Rugby Union Writers' Club in Britain. I am one of a handful of New Zealanders to be members. Because of the distance I don't do much as a member. But I'm always pleased to receive the club newsletters, which sometimes offer hints at what the British writers really think about the state of world rugby.

For example, Mick Cleary of The Daily Telegraph in London may have written that the All Blacks have a reputation as "chokers" at World Cup level, but did the Rugby Union Writers' Club perhaps offer a more realistic attitude among its members with this snippet its 2007 annual report: "The RUWC dinner last January again attracted a sell-out attendance. We are already planning for the 2008 dinner in the knowledge that the winner of our annual Player of the Year award will probably come from the 2007 World Cup winning team. To cut costs, hopefully he's from north of the equator. Or does anyone have contacts at Air New Zealand?"

Mitch-Speak

In the build-up to and throughout the 2003 World Cup many Kiwis were confused by the way John Mitchell spoke. His utterances became known as "Mitch-speak", but the curious way the All Black coach used the Queen's English might have been called "rugby non speak", "rugby babble", "Stengel-ese", or "speaking in tongues".

However, as the *New Zealand Herald* said late in the year: "His manner of speaking was nothing a good interpreter couldn't fix."

Here is a glossary of terms from the John Mitchell dictionary:

A **ABSORB** – "We showed we can absorb a lot under pressure today" – *JM after the New Zealand-Wales test, Sydney, November 11, 2003.*

   ACCURACY – "We intend to make the team strong in accuracy" – *JM at the announcement of All Black team, Wellington, June 2003.*

   ACCOUNTABILITY – "The accountability is back with the team now" – *JM at the announcement of the All Black team to play France, Melbourne, November 18, 2003.*

B **BAROMETER** – "Ali Williams' barometer is his enthusiasm" – *JM after Williams' comeback game against Tonga, Brisbane, November 2003.*

   BLOCK-BUILDING – "This team is in a block-building process" – *JM in June 2003, after the All Blacks played England.*

   BREACHED – "We breached a lot today, which is really encouraging" – *JM after the New Zealand-Italy test, Melbourne, October 2003.*

C **CHANNEL** – "His channel can't afford to leak" – *JM's job description of a first five-eighth to Phil Gifford on Radio Sport, July 2003.*

   CHEMISTRY – "The team's chemistry is phenomenal" – *JM during an interview with Bernadine Oliver-Kerby, Melbourne, October 2003.*

   CUT THE CAKE – "We must cut the cake with this All Black team and good players will miss out" – *JM after the announcement of the All Blacks to play France in Christchurch, June 2003.*

D **DE-CLUTTER** – "When I get the team from Super 12 play, I have to de-clutter their team cultures" – *JM after the announcement of the first All Black team, May 26, 2003.*

DEFENCE COMPLIANCE –"Defence compliance is going to be important to us this year" – *JM after the All Black team was announced, Wellington, May 26, 2003.*

DOMINANT TACKLER – "Corey Flynn is a very dominant tackler" – *JM at the World Cup team announcement, August 2003.*

DRIVERS –"On the field today we had discussions with our drivers" – *JM after the Tonga test, Brisbane 2003.*

E **EXECUTED** –"We executed quite well today" – *JM after New Zealand-Tonga test, Brisbane, 2003.*

EXECUTION – "Our execution was poor today, we did not deserve to win" – *JM after the loss to Australia, November 2003.*

EVOLVEMENT – "[With Corey Flynn] we see the evolvement of a different type of hooker" – *JM when the All Black World Cup team was announced, August 2003.*

F **FAITH** – "I have faith in the whole squad" – *JM's way of saying: "I will have a policy of rotation in team selection."*

FLEAS – To be fair this was actually a description of the news media given by JM's co-selector Mark Shaw, October 2003, but it deserves a place here. *(See also lizards)*

FULFILMENT AND GROWTH – "I saw fulfilment and growth after the hiccup [of losing] at Sydney last year" – *JM, quoted in Australian Rugby Review, preview edition, 2002.*

G **GRADUATE** – "We've graduated Aaron's foot injury" – *JM at a press conference in Melbourne, October 2003.*

GRINDS – "We have to be able to win our grinds" – *JM talks about winning tough games after the New Zealand-Australia encounter, Auckland, August 2003.*

GROUPING – "Reuben is strong in his grouping on the field" – *JM describing the play of his captain.*

H **HILL** – "Richie McCaw is the Richard Hill of our team" – *JM at Brisbane after the New Zealand-Tonga test, Brisbane, November, 2003.*

HEMISPHERE (SOUTHERN) – "[The All Blacks team] now has the opportunity to carry the southern hemisphere flag" – *JM discussing the (meaningless) World Cup game to decide third place.*

John Mitchell — unique turn of phrase.

I **INCHES** – "We didn't win the inches on the tackle line" – *JM after the New Zealand-Australia test, Sydney, November 2003.*

IMMATURITY – "Immaturity cost us the Cup" – *JM after the All Blacks beat France in the (meaningless) third-place match, November 20, 2003.*

IRRELEVANT – "That is irrelevant to us" – *JM when asked on the team's arrival in Australia why they had maintained such a low profile before arriving.*

J **JUNE-WORK** – "We've been looking at our June-work" – *JM summarising the first tests played by his 2003 All Blacks.*

JOURNEY – *the word JM used constantly to describe the games ahead to the World Cup, and the passing of the months leading up to it. It became his trademark description of the 2003 season.*

K **KEITH** – "That's a good question, Keith" – *Heard from JM several times on the Sky TV live telecast at the press conference after the announcement of the first All Black squad in Wellington, May 26, thus making Quinn endure countless barbs from his media colleagues about being "up Mitchell's bum!"*

L **LINE OF DETAIL** – "No differential lies between the line of detail" – *JM in June 2003, to a mystified press group.*

LIZARDS – *reporters, writers, men and women of the media. A common expression used around JM's All Blacks in 2003. (See also fleas)*

LOYALTY – "Loyalty is a great word, but it does not exist in professional sport. It is what the players offer now and what we want now" – *JM after his second squad selection, July 6, 2003.*

M **MIX** – "We're happy with the mix" – *JM on the blend of players in his team at the announcement of the World Cup squad, Ponsonby Rugby Club, Auckland, August 2003.*

N **NUMBER SIX** – "Is he the number six? I've never heard of him" – *JM after the Wales-New Zealand test when asked, "Have you ever heard of Shane Williams?" Williams was actually the exhilarating number 14, while number six was the outstanding Jonathan Thomas.*

O **OUTCOME** – "If the preparation is right the outcome will take care of itself" – *a quote repeated often by JM in 2002-2003.*

P **PREDICTABLE** – "Anton's become too predictable in his lines this season" – *JM after dropping Anton Oliver, in July 2003.*

PROCESS – "We're focused on the process, not the outcome" – *JM after the New Zealand-Tonga test, Brisbane, 2003.*

PRODUCTIVE – "We have 28 productive players in this team at the moment" (two were injured) – *JM after the New Zealand-Tonga test, Brisbane, 2003.*

Q **QUANTITY** – "The quantity of work offered by Anton hasn't been good so far" – *JM to Phil Gifford, on Radio Sport, July 8, 2003.*

QUALITY YOUTH – "We have quality youth in our team" – *JM interview with Keith Quinn, Terrace Downs, September, 2003.*

R **REST AND REHABILITATION** – *JM's description of those left out of the team to tour Europe at the end of 2002.*

RELOAD – "We are here to reload the fitness of the team" – *JM interview with Keith Quinn, Terrace Downs, September, 2003.*

S **SKILL HABITS** – "We think [Andrew] Mehrtens should work on his skill habits". *(Also "skill shifts" and "skill sets", uttered about other players at times during the year.)*

SALVAGE – "The game against France is important because there's now something to salvage for" – *JM at press conference, Melbourne, November 18, 2003.*

SHARED – "I've shared about [this topic] before" – *JM talking about rucking the night after the All Blacks-Wales test, Melbourne, November 2, 2003. (Published in the* Daily Telegraph *November 6 and described as "one of the most incomprehensible examples of coach-speak at the tournament".)*

SLOW-BALL – "There was a lot of slow-ball, which ends up as being no-ball" – *JM after All Blacks-Australia test, Sydney, November 15, 2003.*

T **TACKLE LINES** – "We've been disappointed with Anton's tackle lines this season" – *JM after dropping Anton Oliver, August, 2003.*

TIER OF TALENT – "There is a tier of talent who we want to grow" – *JM before the 2002 end-of-year tour.*

TRIANGLE – "It's hard when you lose a triangle of experience like that" – *JM on Sky TV Steinlager Awards, November 27, 2003. (He was possibly referring to Tana Umaga, Chris Jack and Justin Marshall.)*

U **UNKNOWN QUANTITY** – "An unknown quantity is a dangerous animal" – *JM after the announcement of his first squad for the 2003 season.*

V **VISION** – "Clearly we have a vision" – *JM interview with Keith Quinn, Terrace Downs, September 2003.*

W **WIDER GROUP** – "He has not been included in the All Blacks squad but instead he's gone into our wider group" – *JM's description of players he had dropped from his All Black team.*

X **X-FACTOR** – "I think Reuben's got it" – *JM's response to a question at a press conference, Auckland, 2003.*

Y **YOUTHFUL VIGOUR APLENTY** – "This year's All Blacks will have youthful vigour aplenty" – *JM in interview with Keith Quinn, Terrance Downs, September 2003.*

Z **ZZZZZZZZZZ** – The sound of rugby reporters from all over the world falling asleep at the tedium of waiting for more "Mitch speak" specials.

Now it's Ted-Speak

Now for the latest entries in "Ted-Speak", which records the evolution of the English language under Graham Henry. The following entries are from last weekend's New Zealand Rugby Union press release about fitness training plans for next year's All Blacks. To assist the confused, I've added my interpretation of the new entries.

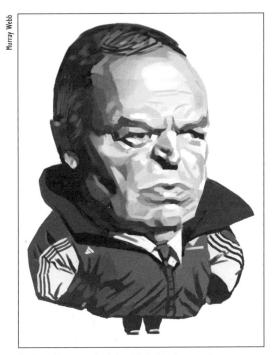

Graham Henry — in John Mitchell's footsteps?

CONDITIONING PLAN — a plan to be used for the fitness conditioning of players.

CONDITIONING PROGRAMME — the programme to be used for the above plan.

CONDITIONING PLAYERS — those chosen to be in the plan and the programme.

CONDITIONING COACHES — the coaches who will instigate the conditioning plans and programmes.

CONDITIONING WINDOW — a window to look out while the players involved in the conditioning programme are bored out of their wits.

LANDSCAPE INITIATIVES — future job opportunities for those players who jump out of the conditioning window and run like hell.

2006

About the author

Keith Quinn has been a sports broadcaster all his working life.

He has attended seven summer Olympic Games and nine Commonwealth Games, and the 2007 Rugby World Cup will be his sixth.

In 1997 he was made a Member of the New Zealand Order of Merit in the Queen's Honours List.

He lives in Wellington with his wife Anne. They have three children and two grandchildren.

Other books by Keith Quinn

Lions 77

Grand Slam All Blacks

Tour of the Century

Disappointments, Disasters and Bizarre Records of New Zealand Sport

A Wounded Pride

The Encyclopedia of World Rugby

Legends of the All Blacks

A Century of Rugby Greats

Outrageous Rugby Moments

Keith Quinn – A Lucky Man

Journey to Nowhere